Bridging the Gap:

How to Free Our Minds
of What Holds Us Captive and Broken

by Jerry Lee Burkert

Dorrance Publishing Co
585 Alpha Drive
Pittsburgh, PA 15238
Visit our website at *www.dorrancebookstore.com*

ISBN: 979-8-89211-360-1
eISBN: 979-8-89211-857-6

Bridging the Gap:

How to Free Our Minds
of What Holds Us Captive and Broken

Content

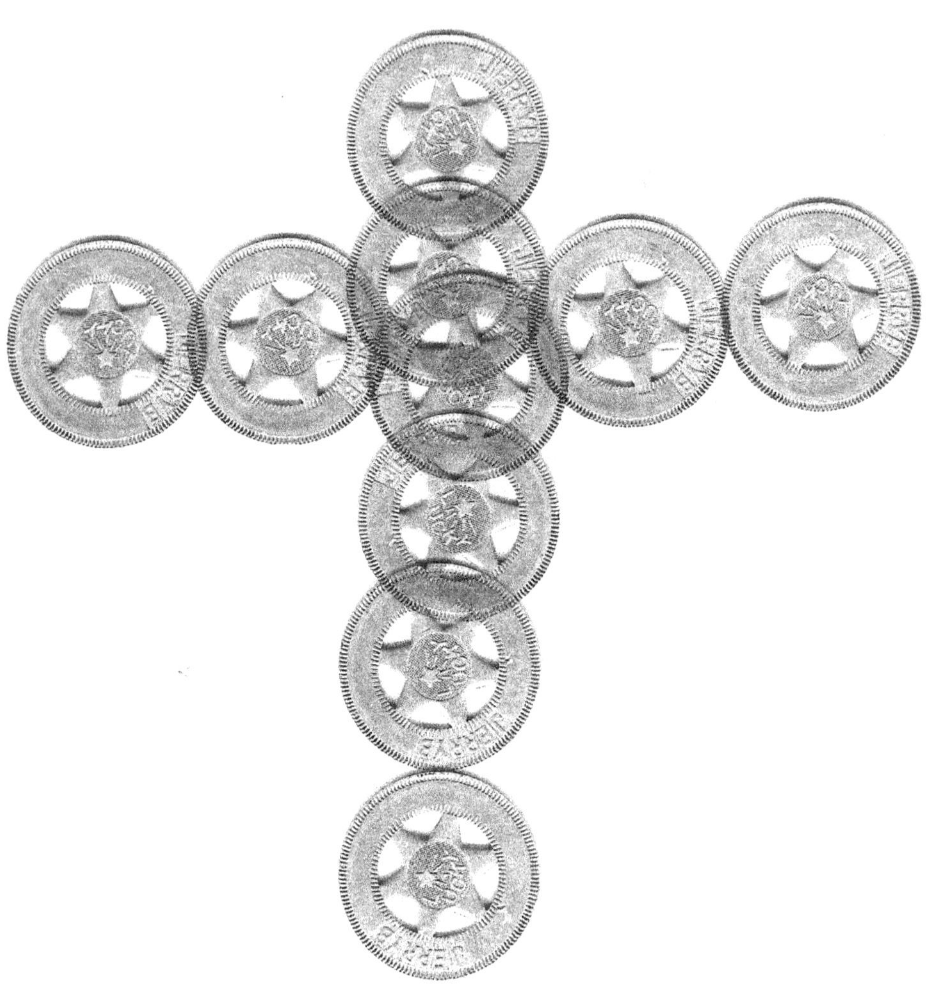

Chapter 1
How life events change who we are!

The year is 2020, when I started writing about my messed-up ways of thinking, indulging in life's escapes and reacting to this life that I absorbed from people around me. My name is Jerry B, and for the first time in my life, I can honestly say that I am truly happy without any drugs or alcohol controlling my life through my addictive personality. But most importantly is that I am still alive by the grace of God, and nothing could be more truthful than that!

I am sharing with you how I became victorious over my old ways of thinking. **"By bridging the gap with my Creator (God),"** who helped me break free from my fear barrier of what people may think about me after I tell you how I was while in my drug and alcohol induced mindset along with the troubles it caused me throughout my life.

This is where I want my brothers and sisters to be standing wholeheartedly together alongside me, as the Holy Spirit helps guide us for our true purpose, which is and always will be, **"UNITY + Strength = Love,"** with blessings from above. I thank you God, our Heavenly Father, for sending all who can now see and feel their inner Souls' Spirit, that can only come from Christ Jesus, whom sacrificed himself for our true freedom and to live out our life in a new perspective. Hallelujah and amen.

I honestly never thought I would be clean and sober for three years, as of September 5, 2017, when I was heading towards my mental break down. Even though this was the beginning of my new journey in life when I started to set myself free of all my false emotional feelings when using alcohol and drugs to help induce my first and foremost addiction, my sexuality that came about from sexual trauma. I never thought of sex as an addiction until now. I passed it off like a football into the dark not quite understanding how this played a major role of emotional feelings related to the trauma that I experienced.

Of course, sexual desires were in our world since the beginning of time itself for creating life, like male animals when in heat they go in search of a female to create life. On the other hand, human males are more domineering when searching for a female companion, and then there are just sick individuals out there that take advantage of the weak due to their physical and emotional state of mind to satisfy their sexual desires without consequences due to the victim's fears.

I was truly never happy or satisfied just using drugs and alcohol. My true desire is that inner tingly feeling that is felt from real pleasure that only the body can be relieved of by emotionally touching another body in a sensual way.

It took me half of my life to understand the truth behind my mind's deceitful way of thinking, which kept me going down that same destructive path using alcohol and drugs to cover up my true emotional being. The drugs and alcohol provided for me as an outside source that I introduced into my body giving me a satisfied but unsatisfied pleasure, but my mind and body were not designed to have false emotional feelings. But once I felt the effects of alcohol at the age of ten and marijuana by the age of twelve literally changed my developing mind into a way of escaping reality throughout my teenage years and quitting school by the age of seventeen.

I was more addicted to marijuana and loved the feeling in my head and at the age of fourteen this friend of mine's uncle asked if I wanted to hang out to party and so I did. We had nowhere to hangout and party so we ended up going to my dad's house because I knew he wasn't home, and I knew we could get into the basement through the outside basement doors that were open. So that's where we went to party and after we were high from weed and buzzed from drinking some alcohol, he said we should lay down and sober up for a while, and I agreed. So I turned off the light and laid myself down on our basement's concrete floor and the only light came from our oil stove burning. I shut my eyes while lying on my side and after a while the man touched me and started unzipping my pants. I was in awe; because I got aroused, I had no control of my private becoming erected, as I was told it was called from my mom before learning it was called a penis. He did this thing to my body part that I had never experienced before in an unusual way, and something uncontrollable happened. I felt this internal tingly, sensational feeling that came literally from inside from where I pee out. I knew what he was doing to me wasn't right, but that feeling was so intense that words couldn't explain how sensitive the body can be.

I never wanted anyone to know what sexually happened to me by my friend's uncle. This secret played a detrimental role for the rest of my life, because I didn't tell my first counselor or anyone of what happened to me sexually, due to me getting off and feeling that rush before ejaculating in his mouth and not stopping him out of curiosity by not knowing any better either due to my immaturity. In reality, he did take advantage of me. Which was the beginning of worse things to come which destroyed my way of thinking, feeling, and reacting in my life as if everything would be okay, when in fact it wasn't.

I was supposed to be sexually interested in females, but this did not occur until I was fifteen years old with a woman that was twenty-one. This was very exciting for me, as we shared an alcoholic drink, which ultimately led to sexually touching, kissing, and feeling the love we both wanted and used each other for our emotional pleasures time and time again. None of my intimate relationships after the age of nineteen were about love, I didn't know how to love. I thought kissing, hugging, foreplay, and mostly, intercourse were showing love, along with using drugs and alcohol to feel more emotionally satisfied. These negative emotional feelings controlled my actions, making up excuses for my drug and alcohol use, because I never shared with anyone what happened thirty-some years ago.

For so many years I blamed it on my parents' divorce, along with my first failed relationship. I was already mentally messed up by the choices I made by not telling anyone about my first sexual experience from a man, which is my own fault. These types of mind alterations from immoral sexual experiences without understanding what love is ruined my future relationships due to my daily habits.

It was crazy for me to think my life was good, just because I was working, had a car and a loan for a house as a standard of maturity even though as soon as I got home, I started drinking and smoking pot before dinner that upset my girlfriend and her children, especially when I played loud music. I did what I thought I needed to do in life as a working man, taking care of the bills and making the woman feel secure in a home and what I thought was showing love. None of my relationships could ever grow into a mature state, since I was so selfish by letting the drugs and alcohol control my life. I thought that getting high was more important than sharing my inner thoughts with any of these girls about a future, which goes to show how immature I was, besides the negative impact it had on these girls emotionally!

One relationship became touchy for reasons I wasn't quite ready for yet at the age of twenty-five years old. My girlfriend at the time wanted to get pregnant, and on this night, we were both drunk and she said she was ovulating. Now me, as a young man, I wasn't thinking about what she meant by, ovulating, and she said to cum inside her and so I did, and she became pregnant, and she gave birth to our baby girl in 1995. She was the one excited and I can't lie, I wasn't excited about becoming a father with all of these responsibilities and commitments that would be in a conflict with my drug and alcohol use. None of us were ready to be parents and I wasn't close to being a man with integrity.

Because of my selfishness and not taking my drug and alcohol use seriously, I didn't even get to see my daughter being born and she didn't give our child my last name. Unfortunately for me on this one evening while I was there visiting her moms' house to see our baby girl for the first time after her birth. The boyfriend of her mom started talking to me about a shotgun wedding, and that alone put fear in me, and I wasn't happy to hear that at all. I cared about her but I didn't love her because I loved making love. I was adventurous and wanted to have sexual experiences with all types of girls. I wasn't ready to settle down which is the boy in me. She had the court system make me pay child support and I got to see my daughter when it was good for her, which was only a few times, but I was glad my parents got to see their granddaughter until she met another man and got married. They moved away while I was still paying child support. I was despicable; my mom paid for a lawyer to find her. Once the lawyer located her so we could see my daughter, she had a lawyer send me a release of my parental rights through the court system.

The family connection is a bond between each other that is lost in a broken home! Since most parents are split up or were never together in the first place, living a single life as I was. I didn't want to be alone, and I had a daughter out of wedlock when she was supposed to be growing up with me as her father and her mom in a family atmosphere as God meant it to be. I was the problem, no one else, and I accept my faults today unlike when I was in my twenties. I had to weigh out the pros and cons for my daughter's life. It was a difficult decision to make. One thought was her mother might use her as a pawn and mess her life up to get even with me as our daughter grew older.

I knew at that moment in my life, I would not be a good teacher for her while growing up because of my lifestyle, and I made the decision to give up my rights as her father. My decision hurt me deep inside for all the years that had passed by, not knowing my daughter and not seeing her grow up as a child and into her teenage years. I had so many reasons to hate myself because of the choices I made throughout my life. I always hoped to meet my daughter one day, and she was fifteen years old when I did, because her mom divorced the other guy and was with another and having her own issues. I wasn't clean and sober, but I was there for my daughter. By the grace of God, I was able to help her when she was eighteen and put in jail for some pretty bad charges because of her bad choices, when they were out there steeling out of cars and got arrested with a pair of brass knuckles on her possession which is a serious offense besides this other time, she was with some so-called boyfriend, and he got into a fight over drugs and his gun fell to the ground and it discharged, thank God, that stray bullet didn't hit my daughter or anyone else for that matter which is a major blessing, and she wasn't charged for the crime he had committed by having a firearm that discharged in a populated area of the community.

"Thank you, Lord, for nobody getting shot and killed over dumb stuff."

My daughter and I became close, and she knew I cared about her well-being and the life ahead of her. Things happen for reasons and thank God they do, because my daughter changed her lifestyle after going into rehab and working her program in recovery before having my grandchild and finding a great man with two children and he cares about her future and wants her and my granddaughter to be happy living a better life with a God given future. I am proud of her for being a great mom to all of their kids. Thank you God, for my daughter making positive choices from where she was heading down a destructive path and found faith in recovery and realizing there is happiness when being clean and sober which is a blessing as a child of God including her being baptized. Amen to that!

I was never really happy until 2019, when I turned fifty, because my drug and alcohol use has messed up my emotional way of thinking, by not knowing how to love someone before my own needs. I was cruel at times, depending on what was done to hurt me, and I got my revenge, and I wish I didn't. Nobody deserves to hurt in any way physically or mentally; it's all wrong and I see that now.

My breakdown at the age of forty-eight years old was the only way for me to honestly want to change. I didn't want to live in misery anymore, because there are only two ways out of my demise, which is live or die. I was honestly considering my own death warrant, due to my deeply depressed state of mind that was full of negative thinking as if my life was over. My sick mind was telling me that I will be going to prison for a long time, due to my charges of bodily injury to my friend another human being that was on the back of my motorcycle when the accident occurred, and my intoxicated level was 1.2 Blood Alcohol Content and here I go again losing my privilege of driving and wondering how I will get through this ridiculous situation I put myself through again, because I don't know when to stop once I start drinking alcohol.

Satan wanted my soul, like countless others before me who gave up the fight. I am a survivor who is fighting the biggest battle ever against myself with other addicts like me. I was searching for the truth, which is my redemption. I knew at this point I needed to bridge the gap with my creator, God, in order to break free from my old lifestyle that held me hostage. If I had not done so, I would probably be dead by suicide. I could not keep on sinking deeper into the quicksand that was destroying me! My mind is what kept me hostage, making everything seem normal and okay with the people I surrounded myself with. We used each other for comfort while doing these sinful acts. I was trying to break away from this pattern before my last accident occurred. I was tired of this vicious cycle I kept putting myself into. Once I started drinking, my mind would change dramatically and irrationally when it came down to making any good choices. Nobody could tell me anything, to stop me from what was in my mind already, and I would not stop until my desires were hopefully fulfilled, which wasn't every time, though I still took these chances in my life all the time.

I heard of hitting rock bottom years ago. I never thought this would happen to me. Boy, was I wrong. It slapped me in the face and broke me down like never before. I woke up in a hospital two times in my life due to drinking; there should have never been a second time. My mind remembers the fun, excitement, and pleasurable moments while hiding the bad memories, which is the deception deep within our mind that was set-up by the Devil the day Adam and Eve bit the apple!

I had a few friends and, yes, we partied whenever we could get together, I kept to myself most of the time unless I was using my addictive desires more than just on a weekend basis, because I would occasionally end up using in the middle of the week and once in a while miss work due to being up all-night mixing in sexual pleasures before I travel home. you know how girls of the night can be persuasive to get what they can out of their prospect before finishing their task that was costly on my end, but several addictions do this to an addict. I had been wanting to change for some time now and to share my life with someone, and this young woman I met online in April of 2017 became my best friend.

I remember one night, back in May, when I was drinking in the garage, listening to music. This was the very first time Charlene and I started talking live on our cell phones. I wanted to be cool, like I was awesome, and I showed her my Harley with the colored lights lit up for her to see, to impress her. I also started it up for her to hear it rumble for a moment and then I turned it off so we could talk. As we were talking, she took notice I was drinking a beer and asked me why I drink. I clearly had no answer for her. This young lady was not like any of the other women I hung out with. She didn't drink nor do drugs to deal with her life, like most of us do who are hiding something, and I said, "I don't know!"

She didn't know me or what I had done or been through, besides living halfway around the world. She showed me more love and compassion without really knowing me or how messed up inside I really was, but she cared more about me than I did about myself. I have the upmost respect for this woman. She helped me get through my darkest days and endless nights filled with negative thoughts while my self-esteem was below zero, I hated myself and wanted to die!

I never thought that my new friend Charlene and I could ever have a relationship because she lived in the Philippines. Ironically, with nothing else to lose, I thought, why not take a chance on a better life? Charlene and I became a couple on September 6, 2017, which made her so very happy, myself as well, but I was still very deeply troubled by my accident and the outcome ahead of me from my drug and alcohol use that literally tore me apart physically, Mentally and financially.

My new girlfriend could see my emotional state of brokenness from the motorcycle accident that occurred back in July of this year, and she did her best to make me feel good about myself knowing deep within her heart and soul that I was slowly but surely falling to pieces. She helped me get through this mental breakdown more than words could say. In the first week of October 2017, I was still lying in bed everyday wondering why I didn't die in the accident. I was mentally stressed out, emotionally weary, and depressed, thinking about the unknown yet to take place in my life and the loss of freedom for who knows how long. I started debating about going to a counseling center because of the mental state of mind that was overwhelming me with depression and not wanting to get out of bed. I couldn't go on feeling like this anymore, it was as if I was dead already deep within my heart and soul.

Charlene kept insisting that I go get help and we will get through this together. Thank God I wasn't alone anymore, she gave me the strength and courage that I needed to go see a counselor and get the help I needed. I knew I had to share with my counselor about the guy who took advantage of me sexually at the age of fourteen and how it ruined my life as the tears flowed over my cheeks and down my face. I was finally free of that shame, anger and resentment and I had to forgive him to get through my emotional trauma.

I wasn't excited about seeing a psychiatrist, but I did to help myself get emotionally stable. I knew I had to share with him how I was feeling emotionally because of my depressed state of mind that was tearing me down mentally due to my accident and any future of a life, if possible after I am sentenced for my convictions. My psychiatrist had prescribed me Zoloft, that more than less balanced my state of mind so I could deal with my emotions of anxiety, anger and depression that made up my character defects. After a month of taking my prescription there was a noticeable change in my attitude for the better and my therapeutic counselor as a suggestion since I knew of God, to make positive changes by experiencing the Church Fellowship and studying my Recovery Bible to become more spiritually inclined and so I made these necessary changes to grow.

Everything seemed to be getting better, but I wasn't spiritually clean yet. I started going to church and studying my Bible as suggested by my counselor for growth. God works in mysterious ways and on this one night I was awakened from this ill feeling of pressure aching in my head besides the chills that trembled me within as sweat started flowing out of me profusely like having the flu. All of a sudden there were memories of these individuals' faces that I had sexually used for my own pleasure and I felt disgusted in my core being from these sinful acts that were recorded in my memory and it made me feel as if I was losing my mind. I went and lay down on the floor in the basement so my parents wouldn't hear me, and I yelled out, asking God to take these sick memories away from me. "Please dear God, take these memories away from me, I beg you in the name of Jesus to forgive me." I kept repeating that several times until the chills left my body and I went back upstairs to sleep, and I have not been the same since I was freed of my sins.

I thank you, my Lord, Savior, and King; Christ Jesus for helping me see myself for who I was, how I was, and who I am today. The blessings from the Holy Spirit that you alone bestowed upon me the day of my reckoning.

You gave me the time I needed for my character to grow by clearing the path and freeing up my distorted thinking. I thought I had now learned how to handle life's ups and downs with confidence in my decision-making. I was never supposed to be afraid to ask someone I trusted in wholeheartedly for advice and guidance, and at one time I wasn't very good at that. But I have come a long way from how I was due to my character defects. When you're not quite sure of yourself, when something is challenging and troubles you in your thought processing, don't be afraid to ask for help, because we can't do it all alone.

I never shared with others before, what I am sharing with you now or I wouldn't be writing this life-changing opportunity for anyone learning the second step in recovery. I plead with you to bridge the gap between God and yourself, as I did, which was my Divine Intervention after years of suffering by not taking heartfelt advice. I have gone through rehabilitation interventions many times. I never finished doing all twelve steps as I was supposed to do over thirty-eight years ago until my recent breaking point.

As a matter of fact, addiction is not an illness or a disease; there is a cure. God created us to share of our emotions with each other in recovery so we can be healed of the obsession to use, and the devil is the one who opened this part of the mind up of curiosity that led us to being susceptible to addiction. All medical doctors should agree, that anything that sets off our endorphins and dopamine in our brains is what causes these emotional feelings that get us happy and excited. We love the adrenaline rush, whether they stem from good or bad intentions!

Remember this important factor, I had to share with another human being what had happen to me in order to break free of this dark tissue instilled in my mind or I would still be searching for what I thought was the ultimate sensational feeling over and over again, never ending. This is the devil's deception through my way of thinking that I must not tell anyone what happened to me on that day when I was taken advantage of , because I knew what had happen was wrong, and I didn't fight off my offender, because I was amused!

I am 180 degrees from who I was, how I was, and my way of thinking was; as a matter of fact, my life has a purpose now with God's blessings. I had to start my life over from scratch, by accepting the necessary changes in order to accomplish my goals in life with God's blessings, and this is how I made it possible.

I stopped seeing the people I used to hang around with, because these individuals were a major part of my addictive behavior, along with resources that would bring me to eventually use the drugs and alcohol again as a force of habit.

I avoided places I used to go to, because that most certainly could lead me back emotionally and mentally into my addictive patterns, which is my behavior, which is a force of habit, since my mind and body also craved for that adrenaline rush of excitement.

Last but not least, I had to change a lot of things that had to do with my addictive behavior personally, of who I was and how I was, by changing the style of clothes that I wore that were drug related, different types of drug related music I use to listen to, and trying not to act out on situations in life that I have no control over while making these important positive life changing, changes that only addicts in and out of recovery would understand.

"Why would I even consider putting myself in any kind of relapse situation when I honestly want to change my life?"

Nobody honestly likes to be controlled by other people or things unless it serves them well in ways that help us get through life, and there shouldn't be a reason to be under anything's control for that matter. It took me half of my life to finally realize I was always controlled by something in one way or another, but not actually think of it that way. I rarely looked at things in a negative way when I was buzzed from marijuana or alcohol that dulled my senses of honestly caring. I know now for a fact that I needed to break my silence to learn to live again. I had to bridge the gap between God, myself, and a counselor, because I needed to share my hidden secrets so I could finally be free of the guilt and shame that kept me in my addictions!

 My way of thinking changed automatically since the gift of life was given to me within my heart and soul. Thank you, God, for everything. I want to pass it forward to help my brothers and sisters succeed where so many times I have failed miserably. I did not understand all of the trauma deep within my mind that kept me stuck in my character defects, and by not knowing how to react calmly to daily situations when my defects of character would act out in many ways to get me through my life.

The reason I am still alive is my blessings from Christ Jesus through God's love for us all, and to help guide all of my brothers and sisters to our Heavenly Father for the necessary transformation within each other to have a positive outlook on life and beyond. I want you to be victorious with me, because our messed-up ways of thinking are keeping us all trapped in our addictive self-destructive patterns, which cannot help anyone in a positive way, which is meaningless and has no purpose in life. I truly care about my brothers and sisters through God, and we all need a positive balance in life, as we were supposed to have from the very beginning with God's blessings. Hallelujah!

My Heavenly Father disciplined me in a way that my earthly parents couldn't, because I was rebellious ever since the first breath of air God gave me to live. There was no one who could stop me from doing the things I did except me! I only recognized my defects of character from my past sinful ways that still come to my mind here and there, and I ask God to take these negative and sinful thoughts away from me in Jesus's name, amen.

One of my most important growth factors was gaining a positive outlook from how I was, by sharing with addicts still using or just starting their new journey in recovery that they will enjoy life without drugs and alcohol as I do. I finally have gratitude, because of **"Bridging the Gap, with my Creator,"** and I am now thankful every day for my inner soul's freedom, which is the biggest blessing of all. Jesus was sent here for the mercy of God's children and to help guide us through these detrimental stages of our lives that broke us down to our lowest level of existence, by freeing us of our sins and teaching us how to forgive ourselves by sharing with our brothers and sisters our wrongs.

God works through people's experiences to help new individuals who want to break free from needing something to escape their everyday life, as I did in my past. Don't be afraid to share what is binding you up inside for personal growth. Changing from what once seamed normal to me and my transformation to a newborn when I got baptized, my life started over as a child of God. When we desire change in a positive way, this comes to us gradually. When the change in our attitude occurs, we present ourselves to others around us more responsively in the likeness of God, as His will for us all to do so.

Chapter 2
My trials and tribulations

My human nature is the same as your human nature. I did a lot of things out of curiosity, whether good or bad, and it was ultimately my choice. I would do foolish things like stealing candy within close proximity to the cashiers as a teenager for that rush of adrenaline, as my heartrate accelerated extraordinarily fast, like pumping out of my chest, knowing what I did was wrong. This is only the beginning of my compulsive, addictive journey as a youth into adulthood. Everything I have experienced throughout my life was subject to what is relevant. There is an honest to God's truth: for every action has a reaction, and throughout my teenage years, I learned from those whom I surrounded myself with to an extent and then overboard.

"Doesn't this sound familiar at all?"

My family was supposed to be a positive influence in my life, to help build my character into adulthood. Well, that fell to pieces due to my parents' divorce at twelve years old and my attitude changed from being more obedient because of my dad, to becoming more aggressive when living with my sister and mom who was lenient to both of us, **(Bless Her Heart).** I started hanging out with teenagers that were like me, where their parents weren't together either by divorce, or some of my friends' moms were never married.

We were adventurous, which sooner or later ended up having negative consequences, and there were a lot. I used to stay out late at night on the weekends and summer nights doing what I wanted to do for the excitement and the rush of adrenaline, because my mom was working third shift. I took advantage of my situation, which was not good, having the town police chasing me around once in a while, no harm or foul until later in my teenage years.

I remember stealing lighter fluid from Turkey Hill in Kutztown and started a fire on the embankment right next to the store, I then threw the empty lighter fluid container on the top of a cardboard box that I started on fire and pushed it out into the stream more so it would catch the current that floated it down the Saucony Creek to where it blew up under the Main Street Bridge, and the cops came and I was caught and taken to their police station, and they called my parents' house, and my dad came to pick me up. Boy, was he mad and yelled at me, **"What's a matter with you!"** Ironically, those words still ring through my head as if there really is something wrong with me. But at least he didn't beat me up which was a blessing.

Believe me, this wasn't the first nor last time he came to pick me up at the Kutztown police station. Both of my parents were helpless and heartbroken due to my bad choices, which were self-centered, self-seeking, without a care of who else will suffer from my actions for that single quick rush that's all about me; forget about you! So even after my parents put me in drug and alcohol treatment centers several times, and my mind was stuck in a rut and would not let go of my past. I was still hooked on people, places, and things especially at the age of fourteen. I was never good at taking advice from anyone when it came down to being helped.

"Help for what?"

My way of thinking was still corrupt due to my sinful nature, which is a force of habit in my mind. I must face the truth and reality: I was afraid of change! I was afraid of losing my friends who were on the same boat as me trying to escape something within themselves. Nobody wants to get drunk or wasted alone, that is why loneliness is one of Satan's darkest assassins. This was the main reason it took me so long to make the choice to stay clean and sober, because I didn't want to be alone without my friends of over thirty years.

It took me until now to realize that addiction is a type of brainwashing within myself; that is what emotional pleasures do like sexual desires, escaping reality with drugs and alcohol along with other addictions that is clearly deceptive mind control, like testing a mouse to follow a path several times to get the cheese and then change the location. The mouse will remember where it went and will follow that same path but will not find the cheese because they are repetitious in their mind. There is no real difference between certain thought processing between us humans and the mice and their cheese test, when we no the locations of where to go to get our habitual supplies to get through another day or week. I am my own worst enemy, and my biggest mistake was never being truthful to myself and being deeply ashamed of my past.

I knew it was now or never that I bridge the gap between God and myself as a necessity for me to change from my old ways and accept Christ Jesus as my Savior to be able to restore my life and live according to my Heavenly Fathers will.

When I was thirteen years old, my sister and I went to church until she completed her catechism classes at Sunday school, and she stopped going to church because she was going through changes in her life. I said to my mom that I was not going to go alone to our church for Sunday school and had a fit because I really thought it was more of a way to control me as a young boy. It took me forty-eight years of my life to realize there is a Living God, and that Jesus Christ is my Savior.

My life's story is of gratitude for being alive and able to share how messed up I was and why these events actually took place in order for me to help guide my brothers and sisters spiritually and soulfully home before our time here on earth ends!

The year is 2021, and as of September 5th I will have been four years clean, and sober along with three and a quarter years cigarette free which I never thought was possible. I am thankful for God's love by blessing an addict like me to be able to join His Family of Prophets, which is a blessing from my Heavenly Father, therefor His Will for me for the rest of my worldly life is to share of how this incredible change took place from within my heart which is God's given soul through our messiah Jesus Christ, and His Holy Spirit gave me this life I never knew could exist within me and to be given outwardly to guider others for their souls purpose. I want to help my brothers and sisters know that they are loved before and beyond their grave, as I am.

I can help you to stop walking around that same old block and falling into the same old routines, but you must be willing to take that first step in the other direction and only look back for reference to help out other brothers and sisters.

I pray for my brothers and sisters who are still out there struggling, that they learn how to honestly love themselves, because you are worthy to be loved.

"Remember this quote: "I was where you were, I used to be, that I was, and now I am free."

I cannot lie! I have taken advantage of people and people have taken advantage of me. We use each other for our own needs in sinful ways, but once you are on the road to recovery things will make sense in a positive way. We all can learn how to live again, because every day is still a learning process for me.

"Nothing comes easy in life!"

I still fight my inner thoughts, because I'm a creature of habit! I had to stop my habits, which made all the difference in my world that God, through Jesus, blessed me to be able to stop using drugs and alcohol, so I can be a servant to help those who are seeking recovery along with guidance to live out the rest of their lives with gratitude, as I now have. Not every day is perfect! Somedays, I fight my inner sinful nature, which are my negative thoughts that are deeply rooted from decades of selfishness that turns to anger at times. This is when I ask God and Jesus through the Holy Spirit to help guide me when these stupid thoughts that come into my mind, and I would pray for growth in my way of thinking. This takes time and patience for perseverance, with the blessing from our Heavenly Father, but never forget our brothers and sisters in recovery and our close friends at church who can lend an ear when you feel weak.

Now the effects of alcohol and drugs are the main factors that heighten the abuse throughout the world. Everyone should realize it's all about domination over others, in one way or another, which keeps us weak. This is one of the biggest threats in our society today!

There are good people in this world who are willing to share with you like I am of my weaknesses and strengths. I cannot emphasize enough that you have to be 100 percent completely honest with yourself and the people in your life if you want to be free, as God intended us all to be within our mind, heart and soul.

"True spiritual freedom is the gift of life, Hallelujah."

There is only one way to honestly escape this brokenness: by sincerely asking our Heavenly Father, " God Almighty, with your Divine Power, help me to stand firm and strong in my actions accordingly to Your will, and to share of my dysfunctional ways with others, so they can see that they are not alone, which helps everyone grow spiritually, Amen." By sharing with other addicts our inner pain and shamefulness that bound us in our character defects which will ultimately free us subconsciously on how we used to think and act. This will enable us to live a healthier life both mentally and physically, as we were supposed to be the day God gave us that first breath of life!

PENNSYLVANIA STATE POLICE
GO# PA 2022-1635697

DUI CRASH COMBINATION ALC/DRUG
ARRESTEE (includes runaway)
1 - BURKERT, JERRY LEE

Chapter 3
My bad choices and the system's enforcers!

In the early morning on July 21, 2017, I was awakened by the surgeon who had stapled my scalp back together on the right-hand side of my head, and he asked me if I would give a blood sample. Of course I was confused. I didn't realize what was going on, consciously or subconsciously, after my head had been split open from whatever it was that it hit first, the tree branch or the concrete from the road, or possibly the motorcycle's handlebar? So, I said, "No!"

He said, "You refuse?" I said, "Yes." Then the surgeon said, "That's okay, we already took a sample of your blood. We didn't need your consent when it was your fault the accident occurred, and your passenger was injured." Within minutes after his questioning me, I passed back out.

I woke up again hours later while this nurse was checking my vitals. I was more conscious now that the alcohol content was down, and my thoughts were clearer from my head injury. I remembered what the surgeon said about my friend. My mind started replaying the event that led up to this point of clarity, where everything started coming back to me prior to the accident. I wanted to know how she was doing and the possible injuries my friend sustained from the accident. I asked the nurse if she heard about my friend and I entering the hospital due to the motorcycle accident. The nurse didn't know anything. The nurse got the doctor for me, and I told the doctor my friend's name. The doctor came back later to let me know that she was in stable condition in the intensive care recovery room. I was grateful to hear that she was alive. I left the hospital a day after the accident because I had no insurance. I called my parents to come get me, but before leaving that Saturday morning of July 23, 2017, I needed to see the condition of my friend before leaving the hospital. I was thankful for that kind Doctor who took time out to get me my friends room number.

As I entered her room, I saw her lying there, wrapped up at her chest area, as my heart dropped inside of me. No words could express the sorrow I felt. I asked the nurse a few questions about her stability before going over to see her, to let her know I was somewhat okay from the accident before I left the hospital. I said, "I am so sorry for what happened," and even worse, I couldn't hug her. She told me she had surgery that morning on our arrival and that her lung had been punctured from the tree's branch. This made me feel even more disgusted with myself because I couldn't stop the accident from happening.

I told her, "My parents are on their way here to pick me up." So I got her room's phone number to keep in touch, and she had the hospital give me her apartment keys so I could take care of her cat and birds until she was able to come home. She remained in the hospital for two weeks. On the day my friend was release from the hospital my parents and I picked her up and took her home.

God knew I felt horrible seeing my friend suffering like that especially knowing that this could have been prevented. I should have never gone on that excursion before taking her home that night. We would have never slid into that oak tree if I had just taken her home after the bar, even more so if I hadn't gone out drinking and driving. The good Lord knows I tried to stop using my back brakes, and, yes, there were leaves on the road. The road was still wet from the rain that was coming off of the tree's leaves after that storm had passed through the area earlier that evening. I still believe in my heart and soul that this accident was my wakeup call from God, but I was being punished for something that could have happened to anyone. Who would expect to encounter a sixty-foot oak tree that had collapsed across a backroad in the middle of nowhere hours after the storm had gone through this area. Unfortunately, my friend and I were the ones who collided into this tree on my Harley.

Apparently, I didn't care about myself, which is truly sad. Not realizing how close to death I was many times over, but this last accident, where my friend could have lost her life, shook me up inside. I don't think I could have kept on living, knowing it was my fault if she would've died. Knowing I was supposed to be in control of the motorcycle and stop in time before hitting that tree laying across the road. I remember everything up until that point, including hearing my friend and I yelling, "Oh my God", as we skidded on the wet road towards the tree and collided with it. A week after my friend was out of the hospital, she asked me to come over to have a few drinks. She told me she was awake the entire time after the accident occurred. She said she called out for me, and I didn't make a sound. Then finally out of nowhere, I just yelled, and then I fell silent. She said a vehicle came down that road and turned around and left!

It was a blessing from above that she was able to reach into her front pocket for her cell phone and call 911 for help, even though she was stuck on that branch through her chest. Thank God she is a tough cookie, fighting for her life and mine also.

The State Trooper could not find the cell phone's location of where the accident occurred. It took approximately two hours for the police to find us and inform the ambulance what road we were on to pick us up and get us to the hospital.

By September 10, 2017, I received a letter from the Berks County Court with multiple charges related to a DUI and accusing me of unintentional bodily injury to another human being. My heart sank. I knew I could be facing five-plus years behind bars because of the point system.

I tried to talk with an attorney from this law firm about my accident and the tree that had fallen across the road due to a storm. He said, **"They consider that an act of God,"** so I could not sue the landowner for not clearing the trees a certain distance along that roadway! There went my hopes for taking care of restitutions and therapies after sentencing. I was numbing my pain up until the 5th of September 2017, smoking crack cocaine and drinking, wanting my heart to explode, trying to take the easy way out, but God gave me a strong heart. Thankfully my drug use stopped because I had to send my driver's license back to the Pennsylvania Department of Transportation.

Within a week after not numbing my pain for over a month my lower back, left leg, and foot from the accident were overwhelmingly discomforted while trying to sleep, and even worse I did not want to get out of bed. I felt as if my heart and soul was sucked up in a vacuum tube within my body, and my depression set in big time. This was when my breakdown started to occur along with thoughts of suicide. Thank God for my soul mate, Charlene, who helped me snap out of that self-destructive frame of mind that was giving up on any future with no positive outlook and no hope to make it through this messed-up situation I put myself in. My fate was in the hands of the judicial system, who cares more about themselves financially than me, a victim of society.

On December 28, 2018, the judicial system made my friend go against me. When she was done taking the stand in front of the judge, she stopped to kiss me on my head while going back to her seat. The woman judge said, "What are you doing? You cannot do that in my courtroom," which was a blessing for me. They knew I wasn't a bad person. I always paid off my fines and did what was expected of me while on probation from other alcohol-related charges prior to this one, and I knew this judge did a pre-sentenced investigation. The black-haired beauty convicted me of driving under the influence, driving recklessly, and dropped the endangering of another human's life. I was still upset, due to the fact that the top of a sixty-foot oak tree lay across the entire width of the road. I was guilty, because of my blood alcohol content they had the privilege of taking out of my body due to their rules! My restitution was seventeen thousand dollars, which my motorcycle insurance paid out to her, and the rest whatever that was sent to the hospital bill.

These mafia-style groups of people, known as the Hidden Society, created this system for their own financial wealth, or they would never have control over anyone if there was no such thing as addictions, now, would they? The system does not stop the problems of drugs and alcohol use; they contribute to these addictions.

The county court houses throughout America alone make more money than the mafia did back in the early 1900's when alcohol was illegal during the Prohibition years. Now there are so many illicit drugs, like marijuana, that are more acceptable by society now as a crutch for that control.

They take advantage of our society financially, by selling us new laws to falsely protect the older citizens by the control of fear and to keep the money flowing in! Money that is exchanged from one hand to the other is worth more than all humanity throughout the world, which is unlawful and unjust.

This takes us away from who we are as human beings. Why do you think lying, cheating, stealing, prostitution, aggravated assaults, drug dealing, and murder are destroying America and the rest of God's great world? Our old customs of faith in God are what made people tough on what is destroying America and elsewhere nowadays. Negativity must be transformed by teaching and showing how constructiveness builds a positive foundation by learning politeness, being respectful, and honesty, instead of being exposed to negativity by disrespecting, hatred and dishonesty.

If God was number one in our lives along with Christ Jesus, this world would be the opposite of what it is today. The negativity goes full circle, as in 360 degrees, and as you should know from being taught in school, 180 degrees is a straight line that keeps going on in two directions infinitely and does not repeat itself. once the lesson is learned you get what you've got coming, as I did for my convictions, and you keep moving forward!

So I ask you this, why was prohibition exonerated when it ruined countless families' lives in so many ways? Besides, the drugs nowadays are another crippling affect on millions of people throughout our society and the rest of the world. If for one minute you don't think that any of these people working within the branches of the United States Government or any other Governing Rulers throughout Gods world that don't profit from these illicit drug manufacturers, along with pharmaceutical drug companies, brewers of alcohol, sex trafficking and laundering that money in some subtle way, you must be kidding me!

They know how to keep the addicts at bay, by letting their needs be available no matter what or who is killed in the process just so they can keep stuffing their pockets with the hard-earned money of us citizens!

#1. Money = "Big Business" = Government Institutions, State Legislators, City Councilman, Mayors, Judges, District Attorneys, Police, Prisons, County and State Parole, Drug and Alcohol Rehabilitation Centers, Halfway Houses, Counseling Centers on Drug and Alcohol Addictions due to Mental Health Issues from Trauma.

#2. The Unified System = The Appointed = Government Institutions, State Legislators, City Councilman, Mayors, District Attorneys, Public Denfenders and Paid Lawyers that normally negotiate plea bargains to get a lessor prison sentence, last but not least the Judges who send us to prison because, **"The Unified System,"** Is in control, these thieves learned long ago there is more money to be made with prosecuting drug and alcohol addicts besides petty drug dealers than anything else, so who is this helping financially in the end?

#3. The solution = "We the People" = Why should we suffer by paying the price for something that can be stopped before it's in the hands of drug addicts and alcoholics? We need an **Honest-To-God Approach,** in order to have trustworthy, Good hardworking individuals proven to be for the people in all Government Institutions, State Legislative Branches, City Councilman, Mayors, District Attorneys and Judges Throughout the United States of America and whomever is affiliated with Our Country where we have Embassy's with our Allies. With all the technology today, there is no reason for failure!

~~ God will punish those for this account and their associates will go to hell; that you can count on! ~~

Chapter 4
Life before I existed and after my arrival.

The true reality is we are born primitive, and we are taught good intentions; therefore, when I did something wrong, I was scolded or spanked, due to my bad behaviors, as a form of love and guidance to learn from my mistakes as a young boy growing up and to listen when being reprimanded. Our true nature is to be curious of the natural resources around us. We learn by experiencing things, whether they are good or bad, to actually understand the difference! This is a big part of the learning process, which is completely normal.

We don't realize that something spectacular is happening while in the womb and our deep connection from the soundwave vibrations from our mother along with her emotions when talking, singing to music, and talking to her husband that send signals to us in our prenatal development stage throughout every second of her day.

We learn how to trust our natural instincts the very moment we are born. Our mother shows us love before we are born and after our arrival. We were already known and planned for the day we are conceived through our mother and fathers love for each other through the blessings of God. This is how we learn to get what we want. By using our actions of distress when we are hungry, we start crying to get mothers attention. This is also how we feel loved and wanted; we have no idea that this is the start of our emotional journey.

In the beginning of my life, I was a happy, smiling child shown in my pictures. There are pictures of me lying on my dad's belly as a young infant along with my mom and sister's holding me. I was new to this ever-changing world and shown love by my mom, dad, and sisters; as for my brother, forget about it, he tormented me. My mom was taking care of our home and my sister and I while Dad was working two jobs to support his family, as was the way of life for many families in the 1960s! The men from his era were much stronger than these young male adults today, which was for the sake of the family along with their major role of influence on us to help build our characters. My dad loved us so very much and wanted the best for all four of us siblings, and as time passed by, things didn't go the way our dad would've wished them to go, as well as our mother.

We grew up in the small town of Kutztown in Pennsylvania, and it was a rather nice little town, considering it was a college town, and as time went on it was no different than anywhere else with a college campus, where drugs are readily available and bars are throughout the town, which was the money pit and kept the townspeople with more business than they would've, had as anyone would expect!

My dad supported four children, and my mother was a stay-at-home mom, with my three older siblings. My eldest sister, she was eleven years older than me, while my brother was ten years older than me, and my youngest sister was three years older than me, and the year I was born was 1969.

I remember my sister and I used to take baths together as a way to save money on our water bill that my dad paid on a monthly basis. My mom would tell me and my sister to get ready to take a bath, and we got naked in front of each other without any fear of each other's differences, because we were children who were pure in our souls. We loved taking bubble baths as most children do, whether it was shampoo or actual bubble bath soap, which wasn't too often. As time moved forward, year after year, like the seasons change, we obviously started noticing that we had two completely different body parts.

As our minds developed, and our eyes saw things more in depth by analyzing each other's bodies, we noticed differences as in our sex (male and female). As children, sex has no part in our world except for a kiss and hug from our parents or siblings, which is of true love for each other and nothing more.

One thing I must add is that both of my parents had faith in God as they were brought up Lutheran, which is an offset from the Catholic religion if you don't already know that. As children, my parents both went through catechism, as did the rest of my siblings except for me. I went because I was told to go to Sunday school in the 1970s until 1984, when my sister completed catechism, which was my last day of going to church for many years.

My mother and father were born in the mid-1930s, and, wow, what a different era they grew up in. Their lifestyle was simpler, yet they were hard workers and they had even more difficult times when the Great depression happened to my grandparents, not to mention my great-grandparents, who were farmers on my dad's side of the family, (The Reinhart's) that lived in Stony Run next to Kempton in Pennsylvania. My mother's side of the family were from the Emmaus, Allentown, area. My mom ended up in an orphanage in Krumsville, Pennsylvania, with her sister and two brothers because the other two were younger than Junior, so my mom's biological dad fought in World War II in the army and all I know is he became an alcoholic, and there three aunts and four uncles, and they are (The Fritz side of the family). I never got to meet my grandfathers from either side of the family, but I did get to meet both of my grandmothers, Grenny (Mamie Burkert-Reinhart) and Memmy (Maude Fritz-Stufflet) along with my aunts and uncles, except for one who passed away from a motorcycle accident before I was born.

Everyone's family has a history whether it is good or bad. No family is perfect. We all have some type of dysfunctional background regardless of how rich or poor our family is, and there is always some sort of backlash.

I am only human, not God, but a representative of faith through Jesus Christ! I want to help you by identifying through my life's experiences that we all need a higher power. This ultimately changes us from the inside of our souls to open up outwardly, which will help you expose who you are inside and to grow within, as it did for me, towards positive balance in your life, as we were supposed to do from the very beginning with God's blessings. Amen!

My Heavenly Father disciplined me in a way that my earthly parents couldn't do. I was a rebel ever since my first breath of air God gave me. The sad part is my ears were closed to good advice; no one could stop me from doing the things I did except me.

After thirty years, I still didn't recognize my addictive flaws, and went to ask for help. I couldn't do this alone without any support. We are all supposed to work together for a stronger future using the main concept of **"Bridging the Gap for God's Will, Not Our Own!"** We all need some kind of change in our lives to become better individuals for the sake of humanity. I am grateful to be alive, most importantly to share with other addicts my personal experiences as a way to identify with similar issues you may have experienced. I want you to gain the Strength, Courage and Will to move forward and grow within your heart and soul, so you can understand how I got to this point of contentment in my life.

"No human, jail, or institution, not even death could stop me up until this point in my life!"

I should have died multiple times throughout my life, but by the grace of God, I was restored to sanity by seeing my sick and selfish ways. I can now see the truth behind my deceitful lies, and so I gave my oath as a testimony for me to shine like the sun. I will not hold back any wrongdoing for I am free of all that hindered me from my past unless it hurts others, depending on the circumstances!

It's sad to realize when I looked deep inside myself of how we all do whatever it takes to suit ourselves, and how we can achieve that to satisfy our own personal needs and desires. Therefore we take advantage of someone else, most likely because we have been taken advantage of; in most cases we do what is done to us, when we are not in our conscious state of mind due to our past experiences.

Back in the day, alcohol was a major influence on the population whether you lived in the city or in the back country, along with sexual desires and drugs that had taken the spotlight in the early 1950s.

We all learn about life at a young age by different acts of trauma that we are exposed to by the worldly forces around us and we don't say anything due to fear and possible repercussions of telling someone what happened to us and basically we learn how to deal with our emotions.

Our emotional beings are usually scared with fear, shy of embarrassment, or angry with hatred, depending on the situation. When I was at the cemetery right behind our house, which was my childhood playground. On this particular day, I heard these kids yelling and laughing. So out of my curiosity, I tried to sneak up to see what these six or seven teenagers were doing. Once they noticed me, they coaxed me into coming over to them, and so I put my trust in them. This teenager grabbed me, while the other two kids grabbed my arms and then this fourth kid pulled my pants down, which embarrassed me. I started crying as they teased me in one of the most peaceful places you would consider to be safe. As they laughed at me, I pulled my pants back up and started running back home an emotional mess at the age of eight to ten years old.

Some kids are just plain old mean, perhaps it was their upbringing to be tough and they are thoughtless of what they do to other kids to feel superior and they take advantage of the weak kids, but we don't realize how the actions of what happened to us affect us as we grow older and mature. This is important for us because it builds something untouchable inside as God's willpower that strengthens our character to fight back. Nowadays it's called bullying. This is what helps you fight for yourself with your fists, not a gun, knife, or baseball bat, but your own hands like in the good old days, because you live to fight another day!

I remember walking home from school. I was twelve years old when this older boy started fighting with me. I started crying from him punching me in my face and beating me up. This happened two days in a row; nobody stopped his attacks on me.

On the third day this kid, Troy, got what was coming to him. My sister saw what was happening to me. She started cheering and leading me on with encouragement that gave me the strength I needed. She said it several times, "fight back, Jerry, and don't let him beat you up." That is when I started swinging punches and winning, while he quickly moved away from me. He would always be crying that someone younger than him stopped his assaults, and he never attempted to fight me again, because he ended up with the black and blue eye, not me.

> **We all hide our secrets from our loved ones, because we enjoyed the excitement of whatever gave us that rush of adrenaline. I never wanted to admit what I have done wrong personally or had been done inappropriately to me, which I was ashamed of and kept it to myself.**

In the beginning of my youthful experimentation in life, I personally wanted that connection between the mind and body that gave me the adrenaline rush of doing something exciting and new, like touching each other to get a reaction whether it was with a boy or girl.

This is a normal growth pattern at the age of fourteen and getting an erection, since we are young and learning about each other's private parts that have a mind of their own for us boys, which was a new sensation in that time of my life, anyway. I was also a follower. I wanted to experience what others are doing around me, like stealing candy from the store when people were in close proximity, for that rush of doing something I should not be doing in the first place because it is wrong.

I had experienced the effects of alcohol along with marijuana by the age of twelve. I did not understand why adults and high schoolers liked to feel this confusing, mind-altering feeling of wooziness while spiraling out of control, and yet there is laughter over acting goofy. So, as a follower, I went along with them, to feel what they were feeling, which seemed happy and fun at that moment in my youth.

I remember sneaking into my parents' bedroom, snooping around in their dresser drawers when I came across these magazines that had naked men and women in it. I had never seen a woman naked before, except my sister when we used to take baths together a few years back. I was intrigued by what the man and woman were doing in those pictures. I had no experience of an erections yet at the age of twelve. I wanted to know what they were doing naked together and how his ding dong was outward and what she was doing with it.

Many of us have been taken advantage of because we are vulnerable and did not realize when we were being set up, like me at the age of fourteen, due to not quite understanding what his intent was.

When growing up we don't always know why we do the things we do, and when my so-called friend's uncle took advantage of me, I knowingly, out of curiosity that killed the cat per se, didn't fight off my offender. Perhaps, I was intrigued by him unzipping my jeans while pulling down my underwear from in front of my private, which I had no control over becoming aroused by what he was doing, and then this incredible, uncontrollable feeling that occurred. I wasn't sure what just happened, but something within me happened where my mind and body experienced sexual euphoria together for the first time, and this was supposed to happen with a girl my age, not an adult man. I still wonder why I let him do what he did to this day. I let this sexual act occur with no resistance, which actually changed my course in life from becoming a man at the age of eighteen to being a drug addict that was immature and not caring about my future like there was none.

Not long after I felt that sensational feeling, "The bodies sexual high," I wanted to share this incredible feeling with another of the same sex, who was not close to me but willing. I wanted to experience that sensational feeling like my friend's uncle who knew what he was doing when he did it to me out of my own curiosity and fear of what he could do to me if I would try and fight him off. This was the beginning of my train wreck that I did not understand how to stop from happening while I was still so immature at fourteen year's old, learning about life. My own family didn't understand about the full effects that life endured upon me while becoming an adult.

We all become damaged by not wanting to believe what happened was wrong, yet, inside, these portrayers' emotionally demented minds knew exactly what they were doing before taking advantage of us for their own needs. This destroys our thinking pattern through deception, and by emotionally binding us with trust issues, anger issues, or even love issues. I had them all, and learned how to escape by using alcohol and drugs, thinking I would be okay!

There is an honest-to-God truth: from our actions to every reaction, our habits are instilled within us from our family to the people we spend our time with the most.

I had my group of friends and we looked out for each other in ways of support, strength, and companionship. We were not out to take over anything but to party and have fun, since we lived in a small college town. We just wanted to party and play around, not to hurt anyone physically for control.

My life would have been worse growing up in the city.
I need not say no more than that!

I probably would have been fighting against these gangs but then again, I guess you never know, thank God I'm a country boy to a sense. Since the nineteen eighties these groups of gangs muscled there way by force to have control over their surroundings with guns, drugs and violence, and by initiating you into their gangs whether you want it or not, (friend or foe). Perhaps these individuals wanted that connection due to knowing each other and or already are related through the family, since most families are broken in today's world.

Or you don't want to be like them, and they intimidate you because these vicious groups of gangs will break you down as their prospects, literally, then enlist you to do their evil bidding. The perpetrator or perpetrators were victims before you, and this keeps on going like the domino effect.

These devious acts of murder, rape, assaults, and stealing for money are for their own satisfaction which shows no fear, which makes the predators feel in control of everything around them out in the streets. There is always that possibility that anyone can become like the deceitful predators who expose you to their sickness, depending on how you emotionally responded towards the devious act or acts that have been introduced to you, willingly or unwillingly, whether it felt emotionally good or emotionally bad, depending on what has taken place and whether you were forcefully controlled or unforce fully controlled, depending on the assailants' actions.

The biggest threat in our world at large is alcohol and drugs, because it heightens the abuse throughout the world; everyone should realize this. They have been using substances to dominate people since the beginning of time, which keeps us weak and oppressed. This is why Satan's evildoers are in politically high places throughout the world. They want to control you and I, who are believers in God and Country completely out of the picture, because they know we will fight until the bitter end if need be.

We need to pay attention now more than ever and to use good judgement by turning away from our alcohol-and-drug-using lifestyle and start living a God-driven life for the sake of humanity. God's free will isn't free, if we just sit around waiting for God to do the work for us! We are the heaven-sent army; that is the reason our Messiah, Jesus, the son of man who died for us all, has risen as the cornerstone of the afterlife. Our mission is to save our brothers and sisters globally, throughout the world he has created from persecution and oppression! We are supposed to do our part in restoring each other out of love, and when there is love there is no hate or jealousy.

Does anyone truly know what love is?

Most young ladies are searching for a true, loving, compassionate relationship, and young men don't even understand exactly what love is except for having sex.

One thing is for sure: we all have our own imagination of what it should feel like through what we envision from movies, family, friends, and our emotional aspects, but that is distorted by everything that is going on around us and to us!

Nobody truly wants to be alone. We were born in the bond of belonging to another whom we physically and mentally depend on and trust for our survival. This bond is directly with our mother, while our dads are supposed to be the providers, teachers, and the punishers when us kids got out of line, because our fathers here on earth are to care about their children's wellbeing, which was God sent for me.

We all really want alleviating companionship that brings us up mentally, spiritually, which makes us physically stronger by feeling loved and respected. This empowers our mindset to feel positive and confident about decision-making and doing what is best for our souls' purpose, which is God sent!

Not one person expects to be deceived by the individual who is closest to their heart, because we want to believe that they are being truthful, as our parents are or were supposed to be to us while we grow up, and that is a special bond. Sooner than later, we end up looking for the love of our life, which is the most sacred bond between two people of the opposite sex. We are supposed to be completely honest with each other and share who we are along with our weaknesses and strengths, but the fear of sharing our past destroys what could save the future with whom we love.

Loneliness is one of Satan's darkest assassins inside our own minds that destroys us, besides people who deceive us along our emotional journey. No one wants to be alone, so we have faith in what we see, which is often more realistic than something we do not see.

In more cases than we know, the abuse of power and control from either parent is inflicted on children, whether intentional or unintentional, because of their mindset from these memories. We as children are supposed to be loved by our parents and we learn to imitate them as we grow up.

Though The abuse of power from being yelled at, beaten, and possibly molested by their own parent or guardian, who is definitely a type of manipulator, deceiver, and predator. Not all people who drink alcohol or do their drugs of choice take their emotions out on their family in an abusive or overpowering way, because a clear-headed control freak can be abusive in any way for their own pleasures without any mind-altering drugs, which clearly means they are fully aware of their abusive control, which is horrific and nasty either way. All actions presented to us in one way or another affect our way of thinking, whether it's of good or bad intentions, who it benefitted the most emotionally, and how often it occurred, and were these emotions toward us interpreted bad or good, because no real understanding of what we are doing or is being done to us depends on the nature of the act!

There is only one way to honestly escape any brokenness: by sincerely asking our Heavenly Father; **(God Almighty)**, with His Divine Power, to help guide us to stand firm and strong in our actions accordingly; to His will for us to share of our dysfunctional ways with another, which takes away our inner pain that binds our character and frees our true inner spirit, which will break us away from our sickness within and we become righteous and just for the sake of humanity. We live a healthier life both mentally and physically as we were supposed to be by the will of our Creator, God.

If we only understood the warning signs, when they were developing in our mentality!

The sad thing is we don't realize we were damaged or broken spiritually, so we don't search for help even when addictive counseling has been a stipulation to our recklessness and self- destructive patterns that have landed us in courtrooms, jails, institutions, along with being controlled by the system, being on probation and or parole. Usually, we tend to defend our actions, always to suit ourselves by forgetting the ones who truly love us.

I know I never thought about my parents when doing drugs and alcohol. They were always the ones who were helpless and heartbroken, due to the bad choices I made because of my self-centeredness, self-seeking and addictive behaviors without caring about who else will suffer from my uncontrollable actions for that single quick rush that's all about me; forget about you! So even after you and I have been in any kind of treatment, our minds are still hooked on our old lifestyles, habits, and we don't want to separate ourselves from the past. So we look for others like us, and as the old saying goes, **"Birds of a feather fly together,"** but for their own needs.

Throughout our lives we hear all sorts of things we believe to be true from who we consider good resources, like our parents, teachers, pastors, police, judges, news reporters, and friends, until we find out, for a fact, that we have been lied to more than we know, the bottom line is, what are their intentions?

In the early stages of my life, when my parents took me to church, I was already a live wire who couldn't sit still for long. I had (ADHD), Attention, Deficit, Hyperactive, Disorder. I could not keep focused on one thing for too long. I also interpreted things differently in my mind, which led me to not believe in the stories in the Bible that were being taught in Sunday school. It seemed like a fiction story as a source of control, which is exactly what the devil intended by using my mind to reject something I could not see, touch, and feel, which is why we are taught of things realistically, as in what seems to be logical, natural, and in the realm of science, in which we are always searching for something to prove as factual.

I want to thank you, God, for not physically killing anyone, which is a onetime-and-done entity, of life. Instead, I emotionally took my parents hostage by breaking their hearts without thinking of how my actions would affect them. I did whatever I wanted to do, as a selfish individual, and I admit my mistakes. So should anyone, especially if it is a reoccurring symptom of infidelity and wanting to be in control of someone's life in any aspect, which no one should ever be!

If the offenders would truly get what they deserve for murder (not self-defense), they should be sent to hell with a deserved death penalty; perhaps then these jails wouldn't be needed except for petty crimes; therefore, the taxpayers would have more money in their pockets and the institutional business would stop. So any states that use this as a business strategy for the counties' judges and their delegates get a piece of the pie, and no one seems to care! Why are we paying for the inmates to be living in a nice room with four walls and three square meals a day, besides commissary sales, which is a business on its own and a lot of money being made. This is completely wrong and pathetic!

How come when it comes down to a convicted murderer, they can live out their life in prison? I always thought an eye for an eye, tooth for a tooth, give respect you get respect, because we will all get what we deserve on God's judgment day, which is not utterly unbelievable. It makes complete sense, but if their sentence to death is within a short time frame, we would not have these issues that are happening now in America or elsewhere, would we?

This briefing of my life's story is of hence gratitude of being alive and able to share with you how messed up I was after drinking too much alcohol and how this played the biggest role in my dysfunctional thinking that made me do things that I would never do sober. My alcohol use is why these horrible events actually took place in my life. You are my main reason the Holy Spirit within my heart and soul had me open up about my life; to you, so I can help guide as many of my brothers and sisters spiritually and soulfully home before there time is over, **(Here on Earth)!**

As you should be well aware, we are born helpless, and we all die helpless. Another thing we also have in common is the fact that we can actually be free of all that binds us of our sinful nature and to be saved by the grace of God, our Heavenly Father, and Jesus, our Messiah, for this blessing alone, amen.

Through the power invested in me, I can help you, if you really want to turn your life around 180 degrees, so you can live a more content life, in the balance like you have never dreamed of, but there will be sorrow and pain that will have to be dealt with deep inside your heart and soul that has been holding you back and keeping you trapped in your addictions, besides your emotionally addictive lifestyle.

Nothing is easy in life, especially when changing our perceptions of negativity because of our old ways of thinking and doing things of habit, which in time, like anything else we are emotionally connected to will fade away along with the inner pain. You will truly understand why a separation of our past is emotionally detrimental, like a loved one passing away of old age. This is life, and in order for you to start thinking clearly without restraints from the past, you must have faith in God and foresee the blessings in your life, amen.

The year is 2020, September 27th, and I am three years clean and sober and have the will to live, with more stamina than ever before at the ripe age of fifty-one. I can help you stop walking around that same old block and falling into the same old routines, but you must be willing to make that first step in the other direction and only look back for reference in times when helping others, and I pray for my brothers and sisters who are still out there, where you are or used to be, that is as I was and now through faith, in Christ Jesus, His Holy Spirit was awakened within our soul that set us free! Hallelujah and amen

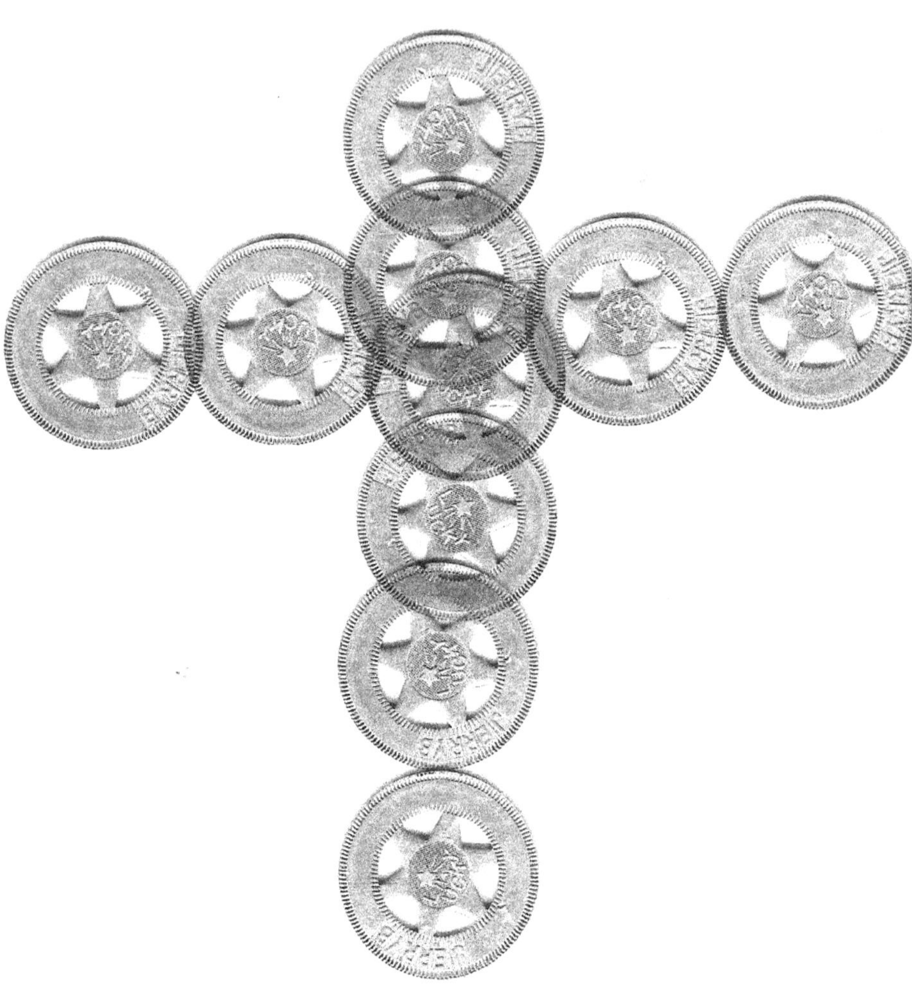

Chapter 5
God shielded me throughout my life!

This brings me back to the origin (post), my motorcycle accident, and this is a short version of my life; in a flash, as my death could've been many times over throughout my years, but this was not God's will for me.

Just so you understand how my sexual experiences and drug use became a major part of my life's demise and dysfunctional ways at the age of seventeen, becoming a daily user and working some part-time jobs, besides asking my parents for money, and I had stolen money from my dad's girlfriend whom I did not like, and boy, did I piss my dad off.

These are the drugs I used from the age of eleven until I was forty-eight, to not care inside from what I had done wrong throughout my life. Alcohol, marijuana, cocaine, crank, all uppers no downers. I especially loved using hallucinogens like purple microdots, mushrooms, blotter-paper hits, and peyote, also ecstasy powder before the age of twenty. I never cared for anything that brought me down, like heroin, which I didn't experience until I was in my thirties, sniffing and smoking it only a few times, not injecting it, but I did inject cocaine one time. Never again, that high is why I ended up smoking crack cocaine for the quick euphoria.

I honestly feel disgusted at myself sharing this now, because I started stealing at the age of eleven, when my parents were still together, so I could go play video games at Turkey Hill and at this pizza joint right up from our house in Kutztown, PA. I didn't stop there. I was also taking it from my mom to go play games at an arcade next to the King's Grocery Store behind our residence at the time in the Garden Apartments. I was a bad kid, doing what I wanted and not caring what my parents thought.

I was a mess early in life. At the age of fourteen my parents sent me to a rehab in the middle of Pennsylvania called Cove Forge. I was scared and angry. On my first night sleeping there, this big kid threatened to get me while I was sleeping, and so I laid awake waiting with the piece of a wooden shaft from the bottom of a crutch hidden under the bunkbed's outer springs above me to defend myself and thank God he never attempted to hurt me because I was prepared for battle and perhaps someone told him that I was lying there in wait, but amazingly enough him and I became great friends after that night.

We did adventurous stuff and ended up getting in trouble for rolling huge boulders off of the top ledge on this mountainside, and we were pushing with all our might when he started slipping along with this huge boulder down this two hundred plus foot drop, and I just reached out my hand and shut my eyes, thinking we were going to die, and I saved him, which was a blessing. My second rehab experience was in a hospital called Columbia Hospital, and I came out of there feeling good, but my best friend at the time said if I didn't smoke pot with him and his girlfriend, he wouldn't trust me. That ended my sobriety until I was nineteen, and went in another rehab called Caron Foundation for thirty days after a truck I had stolen rolled over and I was Medevac'd to the Lehigh Valley Hospital with my scalp tore open and my leg's muscles smashed from the rear-rend of the truck's sidewall frame. The pain I endured was beyond any comparison, and yet I went back to doing the things that could have killed me.

I was a weekend warrior, as we called it in AA/NA, and I only hung out with certain friends and partied until the break of dawn quite often, but there were times I would pass out from drinking too much alcohol and not having any chemicals to help me stay awake, so I would fall asleep in a drug-induced coma until the effects wore off. Waking up the next day, feeling sick and throwing up with a hangover, which happens too many of us at one time or another.

> **"Anything that is mind altering, is doing something to**
> **your emotional state of mind no matter if its PM cough**
> **syrup for colds, marijuana, alcohol or pain medications**
> **it's still affecting your mentality in one way or the other!"**

At the age of twenty-one, I started partying after work, because I could. No one could stop me from drinking shots, mixed drinks, and beers; even worse, once intoxicated, I was on my way, I kid you not. I am very grateful to be alive after thousands of journeys into the city. I used to party in this city of Reading, Pennsylvania, and of course, I knew exactly where to go, as any drug user does, and do what we do, and it's not by mistake! Our sinful inner drive pulls us to go where the most average person wouldn't dare go unless you lived there, and most outsiders would say you're crazy! The insanity is when going into unknown territory, searching for drugs and girls, which is a rush on its own, knowing all criminal activities are taking place because of drug dealings and murders happening more often in the dead of night when addicts run wild in search of prostitutes, heroin, and crack cocaine.

I became more aggressive once alcohol entered my system and I would go into the hot spots in the city for the adrenaline rush of excitement, which led me into getting more involved with using crack cocaine, which was a super rush compared to the regular powder cocaine that took a little longer to enter my brain, which shot endorphins off like a cannon like my first sexual high when I got off.

So, I put the alcohol and crack smoking together in conjunction with the girls of the night and loved the sensual, emotional feeling of several highs. I can't lie how I loved it, even though it was destroying me mentally, physically, and spiritually, holding me captive in my dysfunctional lifestyle, until my motorcycle accident that changed my entire life for the good by seeing what the world is truly like within me and around me as I was running wild with it.

Another fact, this has nothing to do with anyone's origin; we are all victims who bleed the same.

We are all children of God, our creator, and the evil that surrounds us throughout the world is of the ungodly power through Satan's evilness that consumes many lives by seducing us by using alcohol and chemical substances for mind control, which steals our intellectual spirit, which was God-given, and that is our very soul!

Now you will learn about my life and how I changed from a messed-up individual and what created my madness, as in destructive patterns that my addiction caused for me and my family that loved me.

I hope and pray by what I share will open the eyes and minds of the brokenhearted, by healing all of my brothers and sisters from their destructive patterns through God Almighty, so they will find their real life, their meaning, and the reason for our existence through the Holy Spirit only God created through Christ Jesus for us all to change inside for a positive outcome in life. God, through Christ Jesus, gives us the ability to transform into his masterpiece, a beautiful being, whose body is His temple, a head with a mind that retains everything it is taught, eyes to see, in most cases, and ears to hear, to learn how to comprehend everything around us besides, our arms and legs to build off of our glorious foundation given to us the day we were born. Thank you, God, for all of your creations. Amen.

I must first go back to my younger years, to show what occurred as an infant until this very day that God preserved me for my purpose: helping other addicts break free from what holds them captive and broken. By the grace of God, I was saved many times from death to share of God's love for us all. Thank you my, Heavenly Father God and Jesus, my Messiah and Brother of love for sharing your compassion within me for all living creatures. Amen.

I had several DUIs throughout my life, and I am blessed to be able to share with you my dysfunctional way of thinking that kept me stuck in my drug and alcohol use besides having guns pointed at me because of my actions. Once my mind was altered by alcohol it led me to the city to search for crack cocaine and my main sinful desires of sexual pleasure that normally didn't happen from being high, but at least I can count my blessings.

My First Blessing.
My first experience with death was at the age of three, when my dad, uncle, and others were playing this game of quoits, which is shaped like a flying saucer so to speak, with the center punched out in a three-inch diameter, and this object is tossed with a magnitude of force, kind of like a softball player would toss the ball, basically doing an underarm pitch, which is exactly like playing horseshoes.

Now at the age of three years old, I wanted to be involved by picking up the quoits for my dad, and my cousin wasn't done throwing his last quoit. I wasn't paying attention and I went into the pit and was hit on the head, knocked to the ground and my mom started crying hysterically as my dad picked me up as my uncle ran over to assist with this traumatic situation. My uncle recommended taking me to a veterinarian's house who lived not so far away because there were no local hospitals in the immediate area of where he lived in the Pocono Mountains. The veterinarian gave me three stitches and it was a blessing that there wasn't any more damage within me. This was the first of many head injuries.

**"By the grace of God and His love for me, I received my
first true blessing, and there are many more to come!"**

Without realizing it, our own parents cause us trauma that devastates us emotionally in different ways. My parents learned about family life together after graduating from high school and getting married at eighteen years old, and their responsibilities came quickly once my first sister and brother were born, and ten years later my sister and I were born.

When we were being reprimanded, we normally had an idea why we were being punished to a sense, and there were times we didn't quite understand what we have done wrong and being disciplined until they explained exactly what we did to get under their skin. Regardless, as we grow older we act out of arrogance in a rebellious way, which is wrong.

The big issue is without both parents together as it was meant to be, it sets the percentage of their child or children's accomplishments very low to succeed. Without the father figure, there is no real punisher, and mothers are usually more lenient. This greatly affects our outcome in life as the System wants broken families to break America and the rest of God's world. Just look around and see how this happened. Do your research.

**"The trauma throughout my life has affected me in
many ways by not really knowing who I am, from how
I was and to what I have become, "the good, the bad,
and the ugly!"**

The emotional experiences that are developed out of dramatic situations makes us angry, sad, fearful and anxious. These are all different symptoms of being overwhelmed which are mind altering emotions of anxiety that automatically forces us to separate ourselves emotionally, building barriers due to being untrusting of others who have passed negative experiences onto us. Perhaps it may be enticing and makes you thrive for that experience again. Normally, people are silent and keep things to themselves unless it's a group and or gang-related relationships, so everyone is on the same page. We all know when we are doing something wrong in the eyes of God Almighty or human authority.

Sometimes, the ones we think love us can be the most deceitful to us. They use us for their own gain, and many people experience that, which breaks trust barriers. When entering recovery, we are trying to trust other people, which is somewhat a difficult task from being taken advantage in the past when you shared your life with someone you didn't know. Therefore, I kept my distance from other people in recovery whether or not they seemed good for my soul, so I didn't completely break that barrier; due to my fears of exploiting myself to others in recovery, I wasn't sincere. It takes time to know who really cares about us and our wellbeing, except those who show love and compassion. Who else would share their life for us all to be free of what bound us from living an enriched life of happiness? Jesus, that's who, and true followers that have recovered and are still recovering to help our brothers and sisters get through their fears.

We normally don't let our emotional state of mind control us. I know I didn't want that. That's why I used drugs and alcohol to cover up my true feelings because of my emotional distress. I was used to my defects of character that helped protect me, by hiding who I really was in my conscious state of mind, which was broken, and distorted my life's journey until now, because I learned how to deal with my conscious thinking.

This is a fact. If you are a believer in a higher power, you have to read the oldest book from the beginning of time. When life was first being exposed in the light, due to the evil going on from these humans who could see it, and knowing the difference between what was right from wrong, they didn't have the faith in something they couldn't see and followed what their culture claimed was superior until Christ Jesus came into Gods' world for us to learn the truth from the lies of the controlling oppressors.

The Bible helps us to grow in the likeness of our creator, God Almighty, by having faith and learning to trust people again who care about us so we can be truthful with others in recovery, and breaking away from all the things that were binding us in a non-gratifying way and being able to truly love one another as we start to forgive ourselves. By sharing our character flaws and wrongdoing with our loved ones and others close to us, isn't always easy but essential for everyday life, write everything down and pass it on to God, and those of your choosing, as intended for the growth, which is your experience to help others get through their difficult times by giving someone the strength to move forward with God's blessings as he intends us to do. Amen.

Share with those who really care about your wellbeing if you feel distressed, because life isn't easy, and things do occur that bring us down and make us sad, besides feeling lonely at times, which is completely normal. Just know there is always someone in this world like myself who is there to comfort you when you need it, as God's will for us in any addiction recovery program to do.

I pray through my Messiah, Jesus, to You, our Heavenly Father God, heal my brothers and sisters around your beautiful world by taking away their sinful nature that the devil uses to keep us under his mind-controlling substances, which brings back memories of false happiness, especially when we go by our old stomping grounds. Where our mind uses our emotions to lure us back into our old way of dealing with life's issues when nothing seems to be going in a positive direction and we are not yet spiritually grounded, therefore, if we end up using alcohol or any other drug we will be right where we left off in our addiction and worse due to thinking we have failed our creator and the people we love, this is why I pray for my brothers and sisters to be free from their old ways of thinking through the love of Christ Jesus to be healed. Amen.

My Second blessing.
My confrontation with death was from deception, when this older kid named Mark, whose parents owned Mark's Sandwich Shop on Main Street, told me he was going to kill our ducks, and he started running towards Saucony Creek. Why did I tell him that my dad, sister, and I set them free a week ago? So, I started running to stop him, and as I was crossing the street I was hit by a car, a Cadillac at that. Fortunately, I was tossed upward over the front hood, tumbling over the roof of this big car and then rolling off of its trunk to the ground. Once I hit the ash fault, I started crawling to get off the road, but directionally lost. Here I was crossing towards the oncoming traffic on the other side of the street, and those vehicles all stopped, while our neighbor Mr. G saw what hap-pened and helped me get off the road, while his son fetch my dad, who picked me up with his pickup truck and took me to the Reading hospital for a concussion, and my left leg was injured, and I still have a dent on my left thigh until this very day.

My Third blessing.
I had my first car accident while going down to Kennett Square after partying all night long drinking beer and doing lines of cocaine, and once I passed the

point of no return especially when something exciting crosses my mind, then there is no turning back once I was set in motion. My accident occurred on the main highway on Route 30 west, when I slammed into one car that ended up pushing four other cars into each other, besides almost hitting a policeman at the scene when I was actually trying to get away and flea the scene, God does have mercy! I could be spending my life in prison on death row for acting out on something so absurdly foolish believing I was able to locate my ex-girlfriend Vicky, who was my best friend and sex partner, when I had no clue of where to look for her in the first place. How foolish and insane is that? The true insaneness of it all is that we as addicts never really think about the consequences until it's already too late. The state of mind we are in at that exact time of our non-negotiable actions is displayed more often than not, and our actions have negative consequences that impact the ones who love us more than we love ourselves due to our character defects displayed by certain trauma that protected our feelings.

Recovery for our wounded minds takes time to heal. Our past doesn't just disappear. We need to talk about it and share with other brothers and sisters near and far to help each other in a positive way, and this is **"Bridging the Gap,"** uniting us all as one under God and our Messiah, Jesus, by showing unconditional love, peace, and guidance when helping each other in times of dismay by sharing our God-Given Traditional Values that help everyone grow in a positive light, that is necessary for the future of our world that God created for his people to prosper!

The sad truth is, more often than not, most of us have to go back to where we feel comfortable, with the old friends, because we don't know how to live on our own without them in our lives. Sooner or later, without a doubt, negative consequences will occur, and possibly be fatal. One never knows when their days are numbered. I myself, a drug addict who has been in recovery programs several times throughout my life, knows the final outcome remains the same, ending up in jails, institutions, and death unless we change! Now this is when I should have confirmed in my hollow mind that my life is screwed up, due to the negative results that happen every time my deceptive mind along with my delusional thinking that tells me this will pass, which is a lie to myself because my thought processing is still messed up as the day I stopped using drugs and alcohol.

After enough time passes, my mind hides the pain and anguish I put myself and loved ones through, who didn't deserve that sorrow either. I know, for a fact, I do not want to be alone, because it is the last emotional state of mind before indulging in my addictive desires. If I choose to substitute one thing for another, like putting a blanket over my old habits and not sharing with others my struggles in recovery, it will undeniably lead me right back into my old routines, and then I will search for the people, places, and things that bring back the memories that are instilled in my mind, as my good memories of being clean and sober for years could fade away if I don't have faith in God. How sick is that!

My mind lets me imagine that these feelings of using alcohol and drugs with these other addicts like these were the best times ever, even after something life threatening has occurred, and that excitement alone sets off these endorphins and dopamine in my brain and they give me a sensational feeling of excitement which is the rush of adrenaline throughout my body. This is why I kept repeating my bad choices, staying stuck in my old ways of thinking and I didn't fully open the doors of recovery to let the good people in.

My Fourth and Fifth Blessings.
One night, when I was drunk, I decided to go steal a truck from this railroad construction company whom I used to work for as a laborer. I knew where the keys hung on the wall for all the trucks that were in the building, and my intoxicated mind wanted to go on a journey. I never thought about any consequences; my intoxicated mind gave me the balls to do things that I would never do sober. I went there looking for the easiest way to get in which was through the window, and I was in like Flynn, which was an old saying.

I drove the stolen truck to my dad's house and grabbed the case of Saint Pauli Girl beer and a bottle of vodka, then my mind said, go to the ocean and watch the sunrise. When I got there, things went wrong, as they do for me, when you are doing something you shouldn't be doing and end up in jail with charges like me.

I must keep what happened simple. I made it to the oceanfront. I watched the sunrise for a moment and chugged a beer, which was my mission. I left the shore and went to a business parking lot to think of my next move, since the gas tank was all but empty. That's when the chaos happened, due to stopping at a small gas station for gas. I had no money and asked if I could use their phone to have money sent to me, and the store clerk said I could use their phone, which I did, and my parents never answered my call. So I went back out to search for loose change in the truck, and while doing so the store clerk came to the truck's open window and quickly reached in and took the keys out of the ignition, while I was searching under the seats for money, and he said that the police were on their way and that he was an off-duty cop!

I went out towards him angrily yelling give me the keys and that is when I noticed a cop car coming towards us off in the distance. I quickly ran across the street, hopped over a wooden fence into a yard, not knowing there was a Rottweiler in there, which it saw me right away, of course, and it started barking and running towards me, and I never stopped, running like there was no tomorrow, glancing back for a moment with my left hand behind me, hopping up like a kangaroo while using my right hand to pull myself over the fence on the other side of this person's property, which was about thirty yards. That big dog almost caught up to me, which was a matter of seconds, not minutes, and once over the fence I noticed a house across the street with a row of bushes. I quickly hid behind the bushes while hearing a helicopter above also looking for me. The last thing I remember was hearing a cop question the woman who lived at the house if she had seen me, and she said no! I stayed curled up under that bush and fell asleep pretty quick from lack of sleep, besides coming down from the alcohol's high and the adrenaline rush from the excitement.

God, I wish this was only a dream!

When I woke up, I found myself in a jam and searched for my escape. At the end of this road, I saw a bridge, so I headed towards it and while quickly glancing back, I saw the reflection from the sunshine on a white car, and it had to be a cop car making a right, and I quickly went under the bridge, looking for my escape, but I was too late, and the cop was upon me and told me to freeze. I ended up in the Mammoth County Prison, New Jersey. I spent three days in quarantine there and was called the devil by a Black man who didn't even know me from a can of paint, which tells me interestingly enough of how we are all deceived by others in this little world around us!

I was grateful that I wasn't shot by the Jersey policemen who aimed his gun at me while I was running from one side to the other under this bridge to get away. Also not getting bitten by the Rottweiler in that yard as the protector of its realm!

Once released from prison it took me two and a half days to walk home, without food, money, or clean clothing to change into. I wouldn't want anyone to go through what I have been through, but most of it was my own fault after drinking. So I started my journey from hell to get home. Thank God there was one kind person I honestly trusted who helped me out. While walking on an interstate as a pedestrian, we aren't supposed to walk on them because it's State Owned that's why It's a pay toll, which was another blessing. one third of my journey was already behind me when the state trooper, who was a kind Black man, stopped me and asked why I was walking on this interstate, and I was truthful with him about my incident in Jersey and being in jail, so he kindly drove me as close as he could too Pennsylvania. I thanked him graciously for getting me to this point on my journey home before walking towards the New Jersey and Pennsylvania state line that met where the bridge crosses over the Delaware River onto the banks of Bucks County, Pennsylvania where the pay tolls are located before entering.

Once I got to this point, I walked down to the riverbank and looked out over the river, and it was wide, and my legs muscles were in no shape for taking that chance of swimming across the water, and believe me, I thought about it for a while because I was afraid of getting into more trouble than I was already in. I went back up the embankment and started running as best I could across that toll bridge while these people were watching me passing by their cars and beeping at me. I didn't pay any mind to them when I just wanted to get to the Bucks County side right before the pay toll booths and quickly went off the side of the bridge. Thank God I could finally catch my breath, but the pain flowing through my leg muscles was simply unbearable. I was extremely exhausted, but at least I made it to the Pennsylvania side, and now I had time to rest under that bridge before walking again to get home, knowing I still had another fifty-plus miles to get home. God help me!

Once rested enough, I headed back down the road and noticed there was a Turkey Hill off in a distance, and I knew once there I could gather my thoughts and ask someone for a cigarette, besides water and possibly a ride. I noticed this old man who I thought would out of kindness help me out in my situation of being stranded, hungry, and thirsty. I was able to get a cigarette from the cashier at the store, which was nice, and then I went over and asked this old man if he could help me out by giving me a ride home to Kutztown. I said I could give him gas money once I got to my dad's house. He said, "Come on," and not long after I sat down in the seat of his car, waiting to leave, he started reading the newspaper he had just bought at the store, and he opened it to its full width to slyly rub his hand against my penis to arouse me and I said, "What are you doing?"

I couldn't believe this old man was doing the unthinkable and was a predator. He said, "Do you want a ride?" I wasn't happy that I put myself in this situation! So I willingly let him do his pleasure by taking two things from me, one was my pride and the other was my soul, and I hated myself for that.

Predators and deceptive people take advantage of their victims who are desperately in need of something, or are weak from something and are worn out mentally or physically from another like I was.

So after we left that rest stop, the old man gave me a ride to a different Turkey Hill minimart down the road about a mile. We stopped and he gave me ten dollars to get something to eat. I went in the store and bought a pack of cigarettes, besides two hot dogs since I was starving, but as I was exiting the store I noticed he was gone. The bastard didn't help me to get home, and he used me for his own desire.

While writing this, I remember another unthinkable situation a few years prior with a guy I thought was my friend, since we worked at the Kutztown foundry together. I remember waking up from being passed out from drinking whisky, I felt this tingling over my entire body while he was doing his thing on my private. I was not willingly agreeing to this sexual situation, even though at first I started to fondle his penis for a moment, because of what he was doing to me, and then my mind became focused on what was happening; that is when I lost it. I grabbed him by his throat and started choking him with both hands and said, "You're lucky I don't kill you!" I gathered my thoughts, while leaving his place angry, resentful, and ashamed of what just happened!

"What did I do to make him think I wanted him to do this to me?"

I kept that to myself until now because of the emotional experiences hidden deep within my mind that kept me in bondage, along with my other situations and not wanting anyone to know about my past. Our mind tends to put things aside that are not good and out of the ordinary. Here is a recap of something that happened when I was around nineteen years old but never told anyone until now, because I can no longer run away from my past. It sure seemed as if homosexuality and shameful activities repeated themselves more than I'd like to admit, willingly and some unwillingly.

Out of my drunken state of mind at the age of twenty-one, I didn't want to stop drinking and I knew this man from walking around town whom I said hello to here and there when I was a teenager. At that time I didn't know he was the owner of Shorty's Bar, two buildings away from the rental unit he owned and lived in. I knew the man had money, he was not married, and I had heard about him liking younger guys, he was gay as we call it, which is a homosexual. I felt awkward to talk to him and wanted to get more booze in me, so I pleasured him a little to get free alcohol, and because of my past experiences I let myself do the forbidden and wished I never did. I did what most addicts finds themselves doing or thinking of doing when in that state of mind and having no money to keep getting high!

"People use each other every day for whatever their needs and wants are."

Predators look for anyone who is stuck between a rock and a hard place. They know exactly what they are doing by simply waiting if you ask them for something or listening to someone's conversations and watching what is going on around them.

Most addicts know what they are getting into and are down with whatever it is you want out of the deal when being straight forward while buying stuff to get high and proposing sexual desires as a tradeoff, so both share the drugs instead of running wild in the streets, looking for their next fix, which is basically prostitution, due to their addictions as well as yours.

It is truly sad, how sick people are throughout this beautiful world God created for unity, love, and compassion by building lives up, not destroying each other emotionally.

"Do you think this is how we are supposed to live our lives, as addicts?"

We must fight for what is right in every way, because many types of predators look for people that can be taken advantage of and I know because it happened to me several times throughout my life, sadly enough, these were the situations and the consequences that I put myself into because of my alcohol and drug use that controlled my motivation. I felt ashamed, I buried these messed-up memories deep within my mind for decades and now I must set myself free by sharing my secretes with you.

My messed-up memories are what played the most negative role in my life, when I fell prey to another man without my true consent. Like being robbed, this predator, he took my delicate situation and broke my inner spirit even more, knowing I was in my weakest and most vulnerable state of mind. How long had this man been doing this to other people like me when in a des-perate situation throughout his life? How am I any better than he is, since I let him do his sexual act on me to fulfill his de-sire?

I am my own worst enemy because of the choices I made that put me in these situations in the first place. This should tell you something about yourself as an addict. We take advantage of others who are enslaved to their drug of choice no matter what it is that we are dependent on.

Does this mean we are all predators in our own way, so we search for what we desire to feel good which is a power play for control? It is far worse today in the year 2022 than ever before throughout history. God, my Heavenly Father, I ask You, for the power to influence my brothers and sisters in my writing to help me save as many as possible by identifying through my experiences that there is hope when we feel insecure.

We don't know any better when stuck like a rock in a hard place, due to addiction, with no money and nowhere called home to go to. This is everywhere throughout the world. My Heavenly Father God, help me help them in the name of Jesus. Amen.

We have been tainted grey, breaking the spirit's soul, but I am living proof that we all can be healed of our worst experiences by sharing of each other's fears that hold us captive emotionally, by being stuck deep within our mind. Give what binds you away for the sake of truly being free through the son of God, our Messiah Jesus. Amen.

God has always been there for me, but I wasn't always searching to be saved from my self-destructive path.

My Sixth Blessing.

I was charged for stealing a car from a college student, after we were drinking beer and shots of liquor at this bar until it closed and went to his place and after the beer he passed out. I was just getting started because my mind works differently than his and so I grabbed his keys and took his stick shift car out for a joy ride and ended up going over to an acquaintances house where I smoked weed and drank more beer and hung out there until that evening and took the car back from where I stole it from. I had no sleep for over 24 hours and Thank God for another blessing, since I didn't get into an accident and kill myself or anyone else for that matter.

My seventh blessing.

I was drunk and ended up breaking into this drug dealers house. I thought he ripped me off and then again, I was drunk and I was looking for his cocaine stash, which I didn't find. I then decided to steal his stereo system and while doing so his dog escaped and ran away. At least the guy wasn't there and nobody got hurt which is the most important, because one never knows when a gun is around now do they. I received my 2nd felony charge at this point.

> **"My list of offences were rising and I didn't even care**
> **once I knew I was going back to jail. How sick is this**
> **way of thinking?"**

My Eighth Blessing.

I had stolen a second vehicle from the same railroad construction company as before and not thinking consciously about the welding equipment's tanks on the back of this pickup truck that could possibly explode if I had an accident which wasn't a thought in my inebriated mind. Why on earth would I have done such a foolish thing again? I honestly would've never had the guts to take another vehicle again if I had not started drinking whisky. There is no rationalizing when my brain is under the influence of any substance controlling my emotional boundaries.

I went to my sister's house in Bethel Township, PA, to see if she had beer, but she wasn't home. I left there not knowing where to go, and I passed out while driving the truck up a forty-five-degree embankment in a sixty-five-degree turn; the truck rolled over sideways completely, with the bed of the truck resting in the middle of my thighs. I do recall being awakened by a state trooper using a sulfur scent pack to make sure I was comprehending what was about to take place. They had a tow truck lift the truck's body frame off of my legs, so I could get airlifted from this helicopter with a medical team to the Lehigh Valley Hospital as soon as possible back in 1989 - 1990. I wasn't even aware of my body's injuries, though I did get upset when they cut off my jeans to analyze my leg's condition due to it being pinched between the two surfaces for an unknown amount of time, and trying to decide whether they needed to amputate it or not. After I arrived at the hospital my legs started hurting because my blood was finally pulsating through my legs veins again, and my muscles were seriously bruised and sometimes I feel like something isn't quite right with my knees from time to time when going up steps. I let my addiction of alcohol break me down in so many ways, Lord have Mercy.

I remember going into the bathroom and looking in the mirror, and I was unrecognizable to myself. I looked like that boy in the movie, **(Mask)!** I didn't know who I was looking at because that reflection sure as hell wasn't me. My face was swollen twice its normal size, my teeth were broken off halfway like a broken, jagged edged bottle on the upper and lower section center square, besides approximately five inches of staples holding my scalp together, as if a hatchet split my head open, where I once had long wavy hair.

My self-seeking centeredness never thought about how my parents suffered at my expense, I was never thankful enough for how much they truly loved me and stuck by me no matter what I did wrong. They were my blessing from God, and I try to make it up to them to this very day.

I have been chosen to tell my story of encouragement, which is my testimony to help anyone. We all deserve a chance to actually be free of this misery built up inside that keeps us repeating our same old riff raff that eventually puts us down along with loved ones. we all put our loved ones through some sort of grave emotional distraught throughout the years from drinking alcohol and or using drugs. Unfortunately, if we don't realize we have a problem and don't take recovery seriously we may never be able to restore our relationships or even have a chance to make our amends, especially if a loved one passes away before we find ourselves through faith in God, or worse off, never break free of what holds us captive and broken in our addictive state of mind.

"Make amends to your loved ones before it is too late, which means everything to me even though I don't know you, but in some ways, I do, and I do care!"

It is God's will for me to save as many of my brothers and sisters from their sadness, loneliness, that is ultimately leading to our self-destructive path if we do not get the help we all need in one way or another before our lives end.

I have been sober time and time again for approximately six years only because of being incarcerated and caught up in the system that did not tell me exactly how to change my lifestyle. Change is never easy especially when you are young at heart and think you will live forever, enjoying certain amusements and personal satisfactions that keep us from moving forward, which ultimately kept me in my set ways of slowly but surely ruining my life throughout the last thirty-two years.

My Ninth Blessing.

In my destructive path there were a few times where I was very close to killing some individuals over their choice of words from whom I bought this certain drug from. I thought this person was my friend until he made this subtle threat towards me about my girlfriend and our unborn child over this stupid hallucinogenic drug. I was at this associate's house, starting to feel the effects of this hallucinogen, blotter hit, when he said this to me. I got what I went there for and quickly went home to grab a knife, and I returned about twenty minutes later to question his wording. I asked him again what he was implying on doing if I got busted with the LSD and him thinking I would tell the authorities where I got it. This really pissed me off, because I wasn't like that, and thank God he changed his threatening remark to not worry about it. Thank God he didn't say what he said the first time, because I was there to resolve any possible threat towards my unborn child.

My Tenth Blessing.

I also remember getting drunk and doing lines of cocaine at the Blandon House back in the early 1990s with this bartender whose family owned the business; he was a prick sometimes towards me. I had no clue the bartender was a homosexual until that night, when I went with him to this other guys house to party after the bar closed. Once there we did a few lines of cocaine along with a few more beers, then all of a sudden this guy tried to make a sexual move on me, as do all sexual predators when they think the odds are in their favor. I thought, Are you f——n kidding me? I was very angry at both of these men who tried to set me up for their pleasures and insisted angrily that they take me back to the bar before it gets ugly in here. So they did as I wished, knowing I was not kidding around and without much delay, they took me back to the bars parking lot, thank God without resisting my request. Ever since that ordeal happened the bartender treated me badly and kicked me out one time, and I went home, grabbed an object to kill him, and when I returned the doors were locked, and I knocked, and no one let me in, which was another blessing for him and myself. I can't thank God enough for both of these situations not being fulfilled, because I would be doing life in prison, no doubt. The sad truth is these sick things happen every day in God's world, where these wolves in sheep clothing, known as predators, act like they are looking out for you, when they are out for their own needs. We are misled by all types of predators masking their true intentions while acting a certain way to get what they want.

"I was shielded with blessings throughout my entire life from the Man Upstairs, who kept me alive to help me change the way people think of themselves negatively, like their life isn't going to get any better. We are all powerless over our own captivity within ourselves, because our mind plays tricks on us, and this too will end in time. You will find peace if you give your life a chance by having faith in something more than yourself."

My Eleventh Blessing.

A lot has happened to me in the city of Reading, Pennsylvania, over my alcohol use along with drugs and my stupid actions once my mind was chemically altered. That being said, when I was cruising around 10th and Penn Street at night, and I pulled up to this big heavy Black guy and said, "What's up?

Any ready rock?"—the alias for crack cocaine.

He said, "How many?"

I said, "Forty dollars' worth." I let him in my car, and he handed me a pack of Newport's. So I opened the pack and got a piece out and squeezed it to check texture and test it, and while doing this he had pulled this gun out of his pocket and pointed it at my upper torso, because he knew the product was no good. I said, "That's messed up," in a belligerent way and he said, "Give me the money!" So I handed him the forty dollars and he got out of my car while aiming the gun towards me and quickly walking into the darkness never to be seen again. My addiction kept me in search of my cravings even though I just had a gun pointed at me, which is clearly insane.

My Twelfth Blessing.
I was hanging with my one associate, a Black man I met in prison years earlier who injected heroin daily, which was his addiction. I would hang out and have him get the crack cocaine, which I would share it with him and his woman at their apartment room and sometimes I would pay for their heroin, which was the bond between them as their drug of choice, besides survival.

I am not glorifying anything that had to do with my addictions; it is just for anyone who thinks they may be an addict or addicted to something to understand my mentality due to the things I did while using or tried to do for my satisfactions that are negative and can cause consequences in every way. My sinful nature kept me separated from God due to my past mistakes and mindless actions as a slave who was corrupted, influenced, and learned from thoughtless others of that same bad nature, which is always negative, never positive.

Now on this one particular evening when we were getting our rush on, and I, liking sexual stimulation as an extra sensational feeling, asked him if I could have his woman perform oral sex on me, and he quickly pulled out a gun from under the mattress and aimed it on top of my head.

"I sat there on the floor saying, Oh my God, Oh my God, I'm going to die."

I said, "I am sorry," while waiting to not feel my life anymore because one twitch of his finger out of anger on that trigger and the weapon goes off all is over for both of us!

I apologized out of fear and said, "I will never ask for sexual propositions again." That was the last time I ever hung out with them, because I knew I wouldn't get everything I wanted out of that relationship, and what had happened put me a little on edge. I have what many people have, and that is a sex addiction, which is the foreplay up until the final rush before getting off, especially while I was using alcohol and drugs. This has been going on for years, with mainly prostitutes who are drug addicts, so we were all getting what we wanted and that was high and get back to business.

My Thirteenth Blessing.
There was another acquaintance, and yes a black man who's apartment I smoked crack and had group sex and there was always a few girls there or he would get them for him and I to share of our pleasurers with these girls as we wanted; besides girls on girls, it was like being in a sexual fantasy on a weekly basis until his place got shot up on the outside one night when I wasn't there, thank God.

> **"One thing is for sure. I cannot thank God enough for all of the Blessings by accepting Jesus Christ in my life as my Savior, along with the Holy Spirit that guides me soulfully each and every day. My Holy Spirit, the essence of Jesus, lets me see when my actions and thoughts are incorrect. Negativity causes a negative impact on everything in every way against everything around you! Nothing negative is good, now, is it? Once we do our soul-searching, we see the difference in how having faith changes the once-negative impulsive thoughts into positive thoughts; this slowly, but surely as the sun lightens the day, starts a new pathway for living.**

My Fourteenth Blessing.
Happened within a month of the last close call where the gun was pointed at my head, perhaps even a week. I don't quite remember everything to a tee. I was drinking double shots of Yukon Jack while drinking beer until my mind was ready to leave to go find some product. When I was walking out of the bar I saw this little Mexican guy. Being buzzed and stupid I pinched the man's face and said, "You're so cute," and he punched me in the face, and I laughed.

When he came out of the bar, I followed him across the street, snatched his bike out of his hands, lifting it over my head to throw it at him, and slipped on the curb, which was meant to be. He whistled and seven Spanish guys came running up the block to help him fight me. Then, while fighting, one of them put a revolver to my head and this girl friend of mine said, "Don't kill him.

He's a good guy, he's just drunk," and I yelled at her, "Get away from here, you whore," and a few minutes later the fight broke up due to the arrival of cops from a report of a noisy disturbance that could clearly be seen at this main intersection of the street. Then this tall Spanish guy came walking up to me while I was sitting on a step of an acquaintance's apartment building, and this prick kicked me in the head three times and walked away. I was the only one who got arrested for public drunkenness/disorderly conduct.

My Fifteenth Blessing.
Thank God I never ended up with a fatal venereal disease from all of the different ladies that I was with and yes, I was afraid of that outcome when I was tested for human immunodeficiency virus years ago. But I ended up with the fear again because I was married now, and this would change the course of my entire life especially knowing that I could never make love to my wife or have another child all because I wanted to smoke crack cocaine with an old acquaintance that I knew for over 25 years and would get good product with ease.

I knew she had **"HIV - AIDS"**. I went there twice and on the second night there while smoking she asked me to feel under her arm and I felt a pimple like lump and when I looked at my index finger there was blood on it and I said your bleeding and she said it was from bed bugs and I just smeared it on a paper towel that I was using and continued to take another hit not thinking whether or not about any blood ending up on my stem because I didn't pay no mind due to being extremely high at the time.

So I just recently had an AIDS test done in February 2024 and thank God all was good. My Dr. said, you should know better than that and she was one hundred percent correct. I can't fathom how I would explain that to my wife, because we didn't have sex or anything like that but that blood alone could have infected me through a soar in my mouth, but thank God I go to the dentist and take care of myself. I am now moving on in my life for the better things to come my way.

**"It is funny how most people don't count their blessings
because I sure do"**

**"You know, time after time of being clean and sober,
paying off fines and whatever else is expected while on**

parole or probation while under the microscope of authority and taking urine tests, I never thought of it as a shameful experience. When it really is shameful."

The troubling fact is that most of us end up back where we were in our addiction, and we will repeat what has already happened in one way or another over and over again, because this is a normal pattern of everyday life living as an addict: nothing changes, and sooner or later our actions catch up with all of us, as it did for me! You will never truly be free unless you walk away from your old way of living and are willing to change your mindset and start all over again like I did. We are all fallen angels, but by the grace of God's love for us, our Messiah; Christ Jesus, has given us wings again if we ask for them!

Don't kid yourself if you think that these Judges, Lawyers, Government Officials, the Federal Drug Administration, Caseworkers, Scientists don't understand addiction; you should be well aware they do! The Government and Scientists have been studying our minds for decades and how we can be trained like rats, which is a form of brainwashing, and by letting drugs come in the cities which keeps addicts at bay in a type of controlling means, along with people getting drunk daily to say, **"Screw it! Who cares about the world around me!"** If you cannot figure out by now why our world is oppressed then we need to talk of who the advocates are from hell and exploit them, so justice may be served cold, because the time is nearing, and we need to fight for the future of us all.

The only way we can do this is by being strong with God's interaction that has been written through me to prove that you are not weak and blinded by the lies we are all being sold! Control is what the elite have over us. They purposely change narratives to the younger generations so nobody cares anymore about the future of what the family bond means. God designed us to protect what is right, just as our forefathers did to strengthen us within the family structure to keep our traditional values alive.

While the elite are tearing down our city walls to purposely destroy it by exploiting all of the sinful natures that were written throughout history by the prophets to conquer the division between us all by admitting our faults and failures we can rebuild what was destroyed in our world by the color of all brothers and sisters to start trusting in who we are as a human race of one body, united for the sole purpose of family and how to work together in harmony, with positive results as God intended!

There is no difference between you and me in our minds, hearts, and souls. We may not look the same in any way, shape, or form, but as human beings we can't escape the emotions that God intended us to feel or understand, like pain. The Archangel was the snake, and his domain was here on earth. By being cohorts, the devil led us into temptations and exposed our emotional state of mind in these days as well as in Jesus's time.

The breaking of the American Traditional Family was the Government that started collecting taxes, which made life harder to live and support the family by the men, who were the providers back in the day. Once the women started working, they met other men, and out of loneliness from not seeing their husbands or vice versa, people started to lust one another and drink more alcohol, besides other sinful actions that destroy a family within, which is emotionally embarrassing, which then becomes resentment, and sometimes the victims blame it on themselves.

I am now in the major leagues with God's top-notch pitchers for my Lord, Savior, and King, there is only one I pray through to our Heavenly Father, God! Who is and will always be our Messiah, Christ Jesus, the only savior of our souls. My Lord Jesus directed me through the Holy Spirit to do what I needed to do and not be ashamed of sharing what occurred in my life.

The truth is what sets me free, and by doing so; God gave me the strength to stand with honor, love and compassion for all addicts. I plan on spending the rest of my life knowing I have saved thousands of people from losing their life due to their addictions. By giving Gods love a chance you will open the door to our creators healing power that builds the strength and courage that you need to succeed where many have failed. You are not alone and yes, you can absolutely break free from the impulsive cravings that so many struggle with daily by asking our creator; God with his unwavering love to take away your pain and to free you of your alcohol and drug addictions. I can promise you it will happen but you must be sincere about your feelings to recover.

As my life goes on to help guide my brothers and sisters into being free of what hold them, **"Captive and Broken,"** 360 Degrees in every direction the wind blows around God's beautiful world with his blessings, Amen. One day I will spread my wings prior to entering Heaven to live eternity with God and our family that have become Angels. I am doing what I am willed to do by helping free my brothers and sisters of that negativity within their hearts and souls and to help them soar in a whole new realm of the here and now, moving forward and to help guide other brothers and sisters in recovery because we can't do it alone and God must be in the picture.

Our moods change a lot when abstained from our alcohol and drugs that relieved our emotional mess, but we must look at the bright side of life. We will truly know who we are in our hearts and souls, and one day we will soar like eagles with Angels' wings, fighting off evil from our loved ones still remaining here on this earthly world. God Almighty never intended any of this to happen to his children, which we are. He has loved us all since that very day we were born, as our parents are also supposed to do. Our parents, who believe in God, are always teaching us right from wrong while watching over us until they see we are going forward in the right direction as we come of age.

Anything that can or did emotionally destroy us is keeping us bound in our destructive negative thought process where only misery comes out of for our entire life if we don't seek shelter under Jesus's wings as God has willed him to do. Because we have a God-given will, we must choose where we want to be, because our lives are shortened dramatically from the delusional thinking that keeps feeding us these lies that go against our true souls Spirits.

The secrets throughout my life are what kept me enslaved to my addictions of sex, drugs, alcohol, and anything else that took me away from my true intellectual being. As I said, throughout my forty-eight years of my life I didn't believe in God, because I thought it was a way of controlling me, and I just didn't care what was being taught to me in Sunday school. I thought I could handle my life without believing in God as my higher power for my existence, but I was wrong in every way.

We will remain forever broken unless we ask God to be forgiven through our Messiah; Jesus, whose entire purpose was fulfilled when He died for our sins on the cross. Positive changes will come, I tell you no lie, that is a fact; slowly but surely, you will start feeling happy inside in a different way like never before. I can promise you from my heart and soul to yours, in Jesus's name, I pray for you all who are reading my testimony and to feel the love that is only given by the grace of God Almighty to me as a servant of His Majesty, Amen.

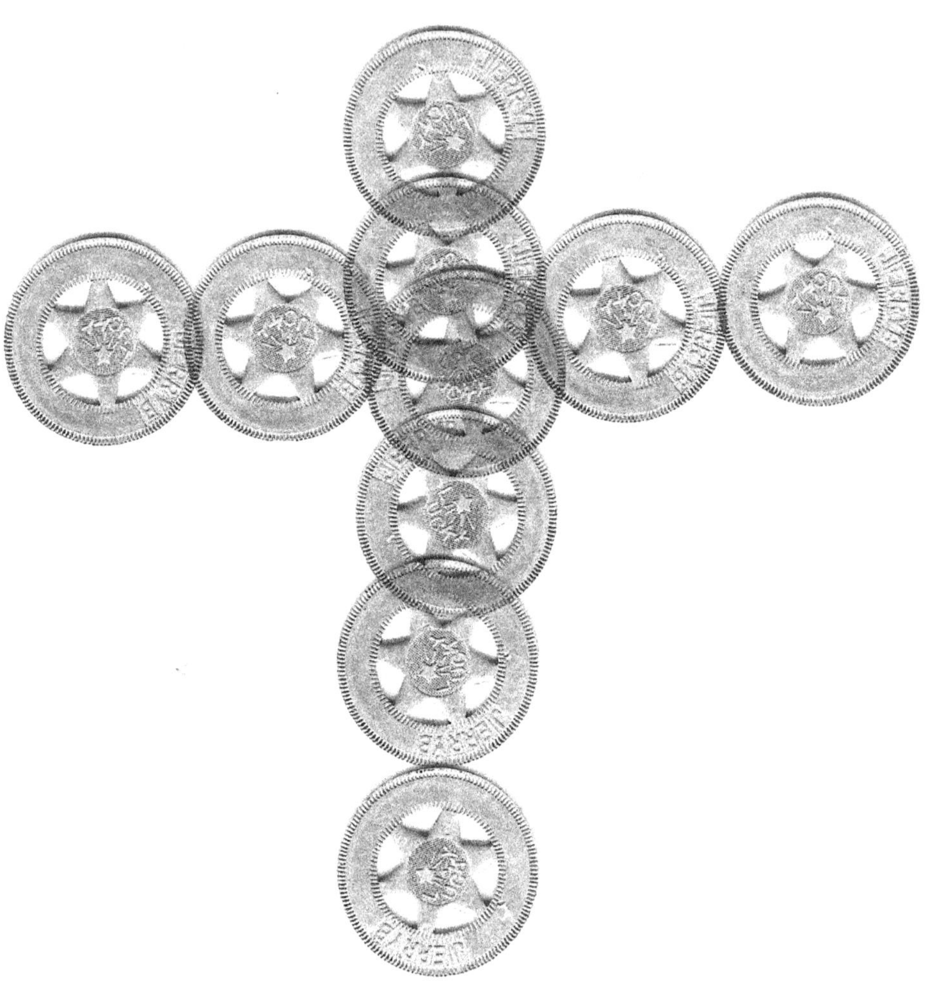

Chapter 6
Positive choices and changes to evolve.

I am here to enlighten you that your soul will fully recover its lost freedom by sharing who you are as an individual by making the positive changes inside yourself, which will help our worldly family rejoice together for that special day when we will gather together with our savior Christ Jesus once again for eternity.

I remembered how I was back in school and how I blocked out everything by joking around and not taking my studies or anything else seriously. This is what made my life more difficult as I got older because my mentality never changed to care enough about myself! The last thing I ever wanted to do was tell anyone what happened to me and the things I had done as an alcoholic and drug addict.

I knew in my heart and soul that my life would never get any better unless I took that first step forward, because I no longer wanted to feel disgusted within myself. Throughout my early years in life being forced into detox, rehabs, and counseling centers on addiction from my parents, through court stipulations and even work to make it look good as if I was trying to help myself because of missing work. I never went to any of these places unless it got me through my insignificant ordeals, as I thought they were, and because I wasn't sincere about recovery when I was never completely honest when telling anyone how I was truly feeling inside.

I made an appointment at this agency where I could talk to a counselor, and, yes, I was on government healthcare due to my motorcycle accident. But for the first time, I wasn't afraid to let the counselor know about my sexual experience to end my fears of being ashamed. I already knew in my mind that I must sever all friends that are bad influences and could never go back, in case of relapsing. I was told many years earlier that I needed to trust someone outside of my old relationships who was clean and sober for a few years and had experienced similar sexual disruptions in their life to help guide me. I needed to change how I reacted to everything around me including people, places, and things, which always had a negative impact due to partying in one way or another because of where I lived or while driving down the road to get to wherever I am traveling to in my area on a daily basis like on my way to work.

Why would I want to hurt the people who really love me? That is what my addiction did, and I am glad that I can make amends to them before my time is up here on earth. My last step was crossing over into unchartered territory by, **"Bridging the Gap between God, Myself and another Human Being,"** and I shared of my embarrassments to free me up of my emotionally bound brokenness that made the tears flow down my face. I knew I couldn't keep moving forward, and the thoughts of suicide came across my mind several times before I had conquered my fears, which was Satan's wish to get my soul. I have conquered my fears, thanks to God and that counselor who actually cared about my wellbeing, for she was a Christian, and that alone gave me the strength to move forward as a member of God's fellowship. I am a warrior for justice and of what is fair for all, and my lifestyle is 180 degrees different from where I was in 2017, prior to this engagement with God Almighty. My destructive patterns with people, places, and with things including music, clothes, and old area hangouts that I disconnected myself from altogether!

Your past will not haunt you anymore but strengthen you once you truthfully and honestly want to **"Bridge the Gap,"** with God's blessings as Jesus, our Messiah, sacrificed himself for the love of us all through his creator the day Jesus was born a man of God's intellectual thinking, mindset; therefore we are equal in mind, body, heart and soul which made Jesus equal with us as His Creator wanted. Infact we are all brothers and sisters through our Creator; there are just language barriers that can be learned by showing compassion for one another. The good Lord knows we didn't find lost relics for nothing, as in the tablets, artifacts, and scrolls that put together the worlds most meaningful read of life's true meaning of how love was a sacrifice in the Bible!

Learning how to live righteously with Jesus's guidance through the Holy Spirit for the soul's purpose is living together in peace and fighting for the good of our brothers and sisters for what is positive for all throughout this world. Open your barrier walls and make the necessary positive changes that are needed, so we can free each other together as one family, by **"Bridging the Gap,"** for the love of one another. We must faithfully trust in this new age of wisdom.

Our unity is the strength we have as a fellowship, an entity of believers who has love if not respect for each other as one world under God, where no one with even a little faith will be left behind as we all work together as one for Christ's purpose, our salvation! I must persist that you give yourself a chance to succeed in your growth towards freedom within one's mind, heart, and soul. I promise in time you will feel the Holy Spirit shine within you, but just know that this is life, and throughout life we have our good days and bad days.

I know for myself, if I do not fulfill my daily needs by accomplishing something positive, like taking a walk, calling someone in recovery just to chat or going to a meeting to be around alcoholics and drug addicts like me who can relate to each other's emotional being. I am starting to learn how to let things go that I have no control over. The reality is, we can't stop these feelings, since we are only human and everything that happens in our life happens for a reason.

"Everything will come together in God's time not ours!"

It took my motorcycle accident and a friend getting physically injured to want to break free from everything that was keeping me emotionally bound to my sickness, of not caring about my life, and stop running from myself and face myself as a man. I was fighting a battle for my sanity against the evil mentality that consumed my inner thoughts and the life it created where nothing positive would have ever come out of it.

This was a fight for my life, like I have never fought before, against the demons that possessed my inner being, which is what kept me silent about who I was, how I was, and why I was like this. It took me a long time to realize how short my life really is, because I was living like I was still in my twenties, drinking alcohol and using drugs at forty-eight years old. I truly believe that God, through Jesus Christ, has made all the difference in helping me change inside mentally, emotionally, and physically and to help others who are enslaved to their addictions as I was.

My inner souls spirit gave me direction in my new course of action by helping other addicts, **"Bridge the Gap with God,"** for freedom within their soul and by doing this I would remain clean and sober, feeling true happiness and love for my brothers and sisters throughout the world that are, going through this constant ever-changing emotional battle within our inner beings' mindscape.

TO THINE OWN
SELF BE TRUE
UNITY
SERVE
RECOVER

Chapter 7
Life without faith as we know it, is dead.

Remember that people come in and out of our lives for reasons, and the internet helps that extremely, if you like a lot of attention, but I was in search of a friend. That is when I met Charlene on the internet, as of April 16, 2017. I never thought at that moment in time that she was going to be my wife on December 17 of 2019, before COVID-19 struck. I can honestly say she was my Angel **(God sent),** to keep me strong with encouragement, to get the help needed to heal within and shine out. I have been clean and sober, moving forward in a positive way while waiting for my sentencing date that finally happened on December 28, 2018; my sentence was one month to a year probation.

On January 30, 2019, I was released out of Berks County Correctional Facility and finished probation by August of 2019. I have been clean and sober now for twenty-three months since September 5, 2017, besides being able to stop smoking cigarettes for fifteen months as of May 17, 2018. Thank you God, for the power to stop what was killing me. Life is never easy when it comes to our emotional feelings. that being said, I was losing my dad, best friend, and hunting partner.

I will never forget how I tried to prepare myself for my dad's passing, due to his heart issues, knowing the inevitable was taking place before my eyes, and, yes, it hurt me deeply inside. My dad was a great man who cared about his family, and he actually noticed the changes in me by having faith in God, and being clean and sober for over two years at this point in my life. My dad also adored Charlene and her daughters, Krizel and Cutiefy. Thank God for video calling and knowing they shared their existence with one another for over two years.

He would joke around with them, and one day he showed them the chicken dance, making us all laugh. Unfortunately, my dad joined our ancestors on my future wife's birthday in August of 2019.

Up until the final days of my dad's life here on earth was when I finally became a man. I did not need anything to escape this reality of what I would be missing in my life from here on out, but you will remain alive in my heart forever. One day of God's choosing we will meet again Dad, in heaven. I am grateful that my dad knew God is with me and empowering me to take my place as a noble man. It was God's will for me to take care of my mom and dad for everything they had done for me throughout my life, especially by never giving up on me through their faith. Thank you, God, for the strength I needed to get through this difficult and emotional time. My mom and I were glad he had home assistance and pain medication to aid him until that very morning he went with our angels to heaven, I miss you dad so very much.

"A man's got to do, what a man's got to do!"

I must admit I never planned for my death, but my dad did, and he bought me a cremation note for two thousand dollars that my mom gave to me after he died; that was when I decided to go to the Philippines for a month to marry Charlene Cruzada. We got married on Dec 17, 2019. I enjoyed our time together, and was sad to leave, but I needed to get back to the United States and find a job to support my wife and daughters. On my flight back to the United States, I had a layover in Hong Kong with a five-hour delay on the 29th of December 2019 before flying back home, and landing in Los Angeles on New Year's Eve of 2020, from there I flew to Newark, New Jersey, and drove home to Pennsylvania. The flight was amazing, I had never been in a jet before until this very first moment in time, what an experience.

Viewing the world from where our God created everything in this atmosphere. I was happy returning back home, because my mom needed my help; it was the middle of winter. Needless to say, I was searching immediately for a new job. It took two months when I was finally called for an interview by this company to be their electromechanical technician, making twenty-six dollars an hour maintaining anchor bolt machinery and brake presses, producing mounting bolt fasteners.

Unfortunately, China supposedly accidental release of COVID-19 attacked the world and forced everyone to stay home. Jobs were lost, ultimately to destroy America and control everyone's life everywhere around God's beautiful world. What was really unruly was the treason taking place by attempt to destroying our great President Trump's re-election in the New Year 2020; unfortunately, the globalists succeeded. People's emotions became somewhat fragile and disrupted, due to being almost held hostage in your own sanctuary, called home and many addicts relapsed due to not having that social connection with their peers!

Then this new and bad administration took control over a majority of the United States, so we the people depended on them for survival by receiving COVID-19's relief funds. Don't get me wrong it was a blessing to take care of my family financially until I got my new job that cleared the roadways for the survival of all essential workers traveling through the winter storms on October 23, 2020, at a salt bagging company as a Maintenance Tech, making twenty- eight dollars an hour for nine months and left due to discrepancies in the workplace the month of June, 2021. I worked at a few companies, hoping to find the right co-workers to connect with, which is not an easy task, too many are smoking marijuana now, and whatever else addicts do. Once upon a time I wasn't any different than they were, until I wanted to change my life for the better.

I worked a lot of overtime at this box-making company from October 2021 to June of 2022 and saved enough money to go back and see my wife after two and a half years of being apart since we got married in 2019, besides filing a petition for my wife and daughters through the United States' Homeland Security to get their visas, and my petition was approved on January 5, 2022.

Now I was waiting on the National Visa Center's approval. I did not want to wait any longer, and I was not working because I lost my job due to my mental state of mind, so I went back to the Philippines at the end of June 2022 for a little over a month, and enjoyed every moment being there with my wife and daughters. We all enjoyed our time together as a family is supposed to, and I miss that bond; it is like no other except God's, and I didn't want to leave. It was comforting having my wife's body next to mine at night while sleeping. It was a great feeling when we all as a family would play around and laugh together.

This was a special time in my life. We would go sightseeing, swimming in the ocean and enjoying our meals together, it reminded me of when I was a child. My heart is sad writing this because my wife says we are not complete yet, and she is right! I was grateful to have that time together with my family, and I miss them so very much every day. Seeing each other on video call isn't the same, and I can see and feel how other people that are going through the same situation as I am hurting inside. I felt like I was missing a piece of my soul the day I had to leave my family behind, where I was happy and content.

This is why, by not having enough money to make ends meet is bad, because I couldn't spend the rest of my life there with my family. You see, these are the things that broke me as an addict even after five in a half years of sobriety. My only true sadness is that my wife and daughters are still in the Philippines. We have been waiting patiently since May, 20, 2022, for the letters from the National Visa Center with a date and time for their hearing at the US Embassy in the Philippines for their authorization of visas to come to America, so we can be together as a family should be. Then I get this letter from the National Visa Center stating that my daughters', Krizel and Cutiefy, visas application went over their due date because I goofed up by not going on the website to read the messages that they had sent to me, telling me that I needed to send my W-2 tax forms, because I sent them my tax return instead of what was asked for, which was my mistake.

My old thoughtless actions took off wildly thinking, Now I had to repay the fees and resubmit my W-2 forms when it showed them the money I had made over the past four years to be sure I was able to support my family, when I have been supporting my family over in the Philippine's ever since we got married in 2019!

I get angry, frustrated and sometimes I feel lonely. I cannot lie I am only human, my emotions are wired differently than anyone else from using substances to escape reality's grip. I am not proud, and I humble myself again. I must remain humble, because I let myself, let go of God for a few months. I stopped reading my Bible, going to church, and I wasn't talking to anyone, including my wife, about how i was feeling emotionally. Even worse I stopped taking my medication called Sertraline, also known as Zoloft, to help me deal with my life better by balancing my mind's sensitivity. On the 23rd of December 2022, I was already in my depressed state of mind and frustrated because I did not have a job, Christmas was here and my family wasn't, I isolated myself from others, wasn't telling anyone how I was feeling inside, therefor I was already in relapse mode. This is how deceitful our minds can be and yes it is baffling how we don't see the obvious within our addictive personalities. Perhaps I didn't want to feel my emotions again or maybe this was God, just showing me how weak I am without him and other believers in faith besides recovering addicts whom have faith.

Due to my sickness that wanting to escape reality, decided my fate for me and so I stopped at this bar in Fleetwood where I used to hang out at and saw someone I knew. Of course, that changed everything. I had one beer that led to shots, smoking cigarettes, and having fun as the addict who cared nothing about the world around me at that moment and time. I ended up going into the city to get crack and got into a scuffle where my money got tore in half, lost my one shoe and rolled my car over on my way home. I received another **(Driving Under the Influence)**, after five and a half years of being clean and sober. I fell flat on my face, and I was right back where I left off, doomed for punishment, for a one night of foolishness. Not only did I screw things up for me, I also messed things up financially for my family, and I really hated myself for hurting my wife, though I am grateful to be alive by the Grace of God, and have my faith, and I will never again give up on God's promises nor his love for me.

TO THINE OWN SELF BE TRUE
UNITY
SERVICE
8
RECOVERY
MONTH

Chapter 8
Have faith and never give up!

I wasted my life without God in it for the longest time and that being said, I wasn't helping my brothers and sisters who are going through their difficult times and being trapped alone in their heads. It has been many years I went back into a rehab to actually refresh myself of what was missing from my isolation and relapse. It has been over 30 years since my last rehab and this was Bowling Green and let me tell you it was not always easy due to a big group of addicts together for the same reasons and still caught up in their old ways of living and functioning to get through everyday life. I could now see exactly how I was as a younger man acting out in different ways to not let anyone know how the real Jerry B was actually feeling; emotionally. For now on I will do the opposite of my sick way of thinking. If my mind says don't go to a meeting, I will go to a meeting, if my mind says to not do something I do it as a way to be a part of everything around me, I can no longer live in seclusion that is not of Gods will for me. I finally understand how my life's daily dysfunctional issues and actions played a role throughout my life. I will now talk about my issue or problems that bother me and how I acted out these issues to learn how my brothers and sisters who had situations that resembled mine and how they set their emotions free which is of the utmost importance in recovery for everyday life.

If you remember most of my story, then you will know that for the last two in a half years of my five in a half years of being clean and sober, that is when I stopped doing the positive thing like going to church. However, I was reading my Recovery Bible and then I stopped that routine along with my medication during the last three months, from October, 1st 2022 into December, 23rd 2022.

I kept to myself, which in fact played a huge role in my relapse because of my dysfunctional thinking of negativity that took over and consumed me with my actions of discontentment, frustrations and isolating myself is but a symptom of being the addict I am and blaming God for my problems and yelling at him for what happened to me and why did he let me do what I did! I was the one who gave in to my emotions and let nature take its course like a true addict would do.

"I believe this was meant to be and everything happened to me for this reason!"

I made a promise and now I am writing what was willed for me to do as a servant of God, by sharing my life's story of what caused the hurting that was hidden inside me, that ultimately took control over my life. Thank you Jesus for excepting me for who I am by regaining my faith in God, knowing he is restoring me to do my part and help anyone who wants to recover from their addictions and to live a life of real happiness in one's heart and soul, Amen.

I will never give up on my faith again nor my recovery and I love helping other people achieve their dreams one step at a time in their new life in recovery along with my new friends I acquire on my new journey in life whether in Pennsylvania, throughout America and around Gods' Beautiful World, and I thank you God, for having a loving and caring family here in America, and in the Philippines who have faith, knowing everything will be as promised with your blessings for the future of this world that you gave us to live on and prosper. I thank you God for giving me so much to offer by helping all addicts with their struggles as I had with my own struggles.

I want to help other addicts in recovery or whom want recovery to move forward past their fears and to believe in God's promises of freedom within one's soul for positive changes. When an individual like me is in recovery and has faith, there is always a glowing light from that believer, whom will help guide anyone who wants recovery but are in an emotional mess because any addicts intellectual thinking takes time to heal up from the abuse we have done inside our brain and these cravings are the negative side effects that make you think things will never get better or that I can't quit my alcohol or drugs, which is our demented minds way of thinking!

I can promise anyone that their life will absolutely get better, when you give yourself an actual chance at a new life by praying for God's help, and this is what empowers you, by relieving the desires to use alcohol, drugs or whatever your addiction may be and before you realize it your remedy has occurred, so you learn to understand through the Holy Spirit within your beautiful soul that Jesus saved you from your addiction through another in recovery with God's love, hallelujah! Amen.

"Once you find yourself and are free of your life's dilemma, your true calling will arise; don't ignore it, embrace it."

Remember to thank God for putting an angel next to you at the right time in your life, like my wife has been there for me to this very day. I do have my struggles because my own Government won't acceptance my family into the United States by giving them their visas so my wife and daughters to come here as they should be able to, but this reckless President who is a scam known for, **"Bidenomics,"** and the fall of America we once fought for, are letting these people from around God's beautiful World cross our southern border all day long. How does anyone think this affects me? I must prove that I can afford to take care of my family before they can even get their Visa's.

I don't want to waste my time on false feelings when in the end there is none, but in the beginning, life moves like algorithms, which flow constantly, because we will infinitely be with our loved ones in heaven someday. Our love never dies, nor does His love ever die; If you believe in God's love for you and I, because it is written, we are all His children, **"We the People,"** therefor we must band together to stop this destruction of life happening before our very eyes as children of God. We are supposed to use the power that God gives us, braided together as one, and we as a whole can stop anything evil going on in America and throughout God's divine world!

"God Bless Us All!"

Thank you for helping me **"Bridge the Gap,"** with you my lord Jesus, so I can **"Bridge the Gap,"** between my brothers and sisters for, **"Unity + Strength = Love**, for the future of this world, especially for our children and we can only do this by sharing of our struggles which unites us from those who divided us on our common ground for their control. We can win any battle as long as we stand together to set the record straight and make the necessary changes to live a free life with blessings from God Almighty, who is the reason we come together every Sunday to worship and pray for strength through the Holy Spirit that will help us band together for the future of our family and our country, in Jesus's name we pray, amen.

Bridge That Gap with One Another, So We Can Break
Free of What Holds Us Captive and Broken!

Sharing something is learning something and knowing this is powerful. God is always there through the Holy Spirit within us to help anyone who wants help with their dependencies no matter what it may be. All you have to do is believe in angels, because we are all around, serving those we love in one way or another to beat the odds against recovery for any addiction known to man.

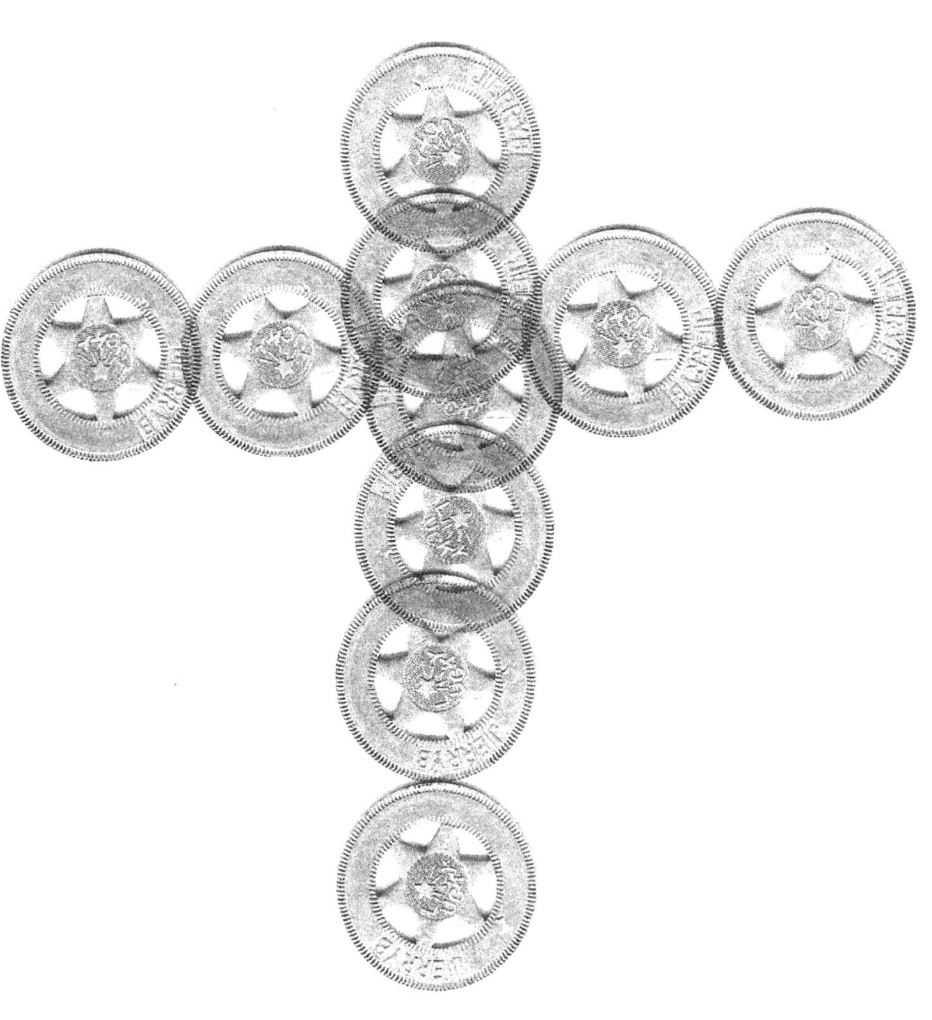